Business, Ethics,
and the Environment

PEARSON
Prentice
Hall

"Think for yourself"
Prentice Hall - Philosophy

Prentice Hall's *Basic Ethics in Action* series includes both wide-ranging anthologies and brief texts that focus on a particular theme or topic.

Anchor volume
Michael Boylan, *Basic Ethics*, 2000

Business Ethics
Michael Boylan, ed., *Business Ethics*, 2001
Patrick Murphy, Gene R. Laczniak, Norman E. Bowie, & Thomas A. Klein, *Ethical Marketing*, 2005
Dale Jacquette, *Journalistic Ethics: Moral Responsibility in the Media*, 2007
Joseph R. DesJardins, *Business, Ethics, and the Environment*, 2007

Environmental Ethics
Michael Boylan, ed., *Environmental Ethics*, 2001
Lisa H. Newton, *Ethics and Sustainability: Sustainable Development and the Moral Life*, 2003
J. Baird Callicott & Michael Nelson, *American Indian Environmental Ethics: An Ojibwa Case Study*, 2004

Medical Ethics
Michael Boylan, ed., *Medical Ethics*, 2000
Michael Boylan & Kevin Brown, *Genetic Engineering: Science and Ethics on the New Frontier*, 2002
Rosemarie Tong, *New Perspectives in Healthcare Ethics*, 2007

Social and Political Philosophy
Seumas Miller, Peter Roberts, & Edward Spence, *Corruption and Anti-Corruption: An Applied Philosophical Approach*, 2005

Business, Ethics, and the Environment

Imagining a Sustainable Future

JOSEPH R. DESJARDINS
College of St. Benedict/St. John's University

Upper Saddle River, New Jersey 07458

Library of Congress Cataloging-in-Publication Data

DesJardins, Joseph R.
  Business, ethics, and the environment : imagining a sustainable future / Joseph R. DesJardins.
    p. cm. — (Basic ethics in action series)
  Includes index.
  ISBN-13: 978-0-13-189174-6
  ISBN-10: 0-13-189174-X
  1. Environmental economics.   2. Business enterprises–Environmental aspects.
3. Environmental protection.   4. Social responsibility of business.   5. Sustainable
development.   6. Industrial management–Environmental aspects.   I. Title.
HC79.E5D4638 2006
338.9'27--dc22   2006036622

Editor-in-Chief: Sarah Touborg
Senior Acquisitions Editor: Mical Moser
Editorial Assistant: Carla Worner
Assistant Marketing Manager: Andrea Messineo
Senior Managing Editor: Joanne Riker
Production Liaison: Fran Russello
Manufacturing Buyer: Christina Amato
Art Director: Jayne Conte
Composition/Full-Service Project Management: Suganya Karuppasamy/GGS Book Services
Printer/Binder: RR Donnelley & Sons Company

Pearson Education LTD. London
Pearson Education Singapore, Pte. Ltd
Pearson Education, Canada, Ltd
Pearson Education–Japan
Pearson Education Australia PTY, Limited

Pearson Education North Asia Ltd
Pearson Educación de Mexico, S.A. de C.V.
Pearson Education Malaysia, Pte. Ltd
Pearson Education, Upper Saddle River,
New Jersey

10   9   8   7   6   5   4   3   2   1
ISBN-13: 978-0-13-189174-6
ISBN-10:   0-13-189174-X

To my mother, Doris DesJardins,
from whom I first learned about ethics and work

Contents

Preface

The starting premise of this text is that in the early years of the twenty-first century, human society is entering into a new social, political, and economic era, "the next industrial revolution." This revolution is being shaped by events at the intersection of the global economy, the natural environment, and ethics. Old ways of thinking about how we should live, how we should manage our businesses, and how we should shape our economies are being overtaken by the movement toward sustainable development, sustainable economies, and sustainable business.

This book provides an introduction to, and an ethical case for, this emerging model of sustainable business. I have had three primary goals in writing this book. First, I hope to bring material from many diverse sources and perspectives together into a single introductory text. The movement toward sustainable business is emerging from a diversity of venues and academic disciplines, ranging from economics and philosophy to architecture and finance. My hope is that this text can unify this material into a coherent and straightforward format. Second, this text provides an introduction to a range of ethical issues that are involved in the evolution of sustainable business. It is often said that sustainability rests on three pillars: economic, ecological, and ethical. I have tried to highlight the ethical questions and challenges that accompany the move toward sustainability within business. Finally, I have tried to do all this in a clear and accessible style. Because this field is fundamentally interdisciplinary, it is important that conversations about sustainability be as free from academic and disciplinary jargon as possible.

Ethics is all about choices we make and about the future we create through those choices. How are we going to live our lives? What kind of person are we going to be? What kind of world are we going to leave to our children and grandchildren? When some people look into the future, they see cause for despair. Given trends in population, poverty, environmental destruction, global warming, exploitation of resources, extinction of species, as well as disease, war, famine and oppression, many foresee a bleak future indeed. When others look into the future, they see infinite resources, indefinite economic growth and prosperity, increased worldwide wealth and happiness. The truth is, of course, that neither future is inevitable.

The choices human beings make today will determine the world in which they live tomorrow. This book is about the choices businesses face in the early years of the twenty-first century. Some choices will make the bleak future more likely; others will increase the chance for a future of long-term prosperity. This book makes an ethical case for redesigning and reconceptualizing business along principles of sustainable development, principles that should make the healthy, prosperous, and happy future more feasible.

Why the need to redesign and reconceptualize business? Several undeniable facts about the world in which we live make this case. First, a large percentage of the world's population, mostly children and the overwhelming majority of them morally innocent in every way, lack the basic requirements of a decent human life. Lack of clean drinking water, nutritious food, health care, education, work, shelter, clothing, and hope, is a daily reality for billions of people. Population growth, even at the most conservative rates, will significantly exacerbate these problems in the near future. Because population growth is highest in those areas in which people are already most at risk due to the effects of poverty and oppression, these ethical challenges will only get worse in the future. To meet these needs, the world's economy must produce substantial amounts of food, clothing, shelter, health care, and jobs, and distribute these goods and services to those in need. Clearly then, significant worldwide economic activity must occur if these harms are to be addressed at all.

Furthermore, an increasingly integrated global economy means that fewer and fewer business decisions can be made in isolation of the social, political, environmental, and economic events happening throughout the rest of the world. Gone are the days (if ever they truly existed) when business decisions in the United States or Western Europe could be made in ignorance and independence of financial markets in China, labor markets in India, or resource markets in the Middle East. Economic activity aimed at meeting the needs of the expanding world's population has already shifted the economic center of gravity away from the United States and Western Europe and toward Asia.

But addressing these ethical goals with the extensive economic activity relies upon the productive capacity of the Earth's ecosystems. Two facts about that ecosystem are at the core of my argument. First, the economy is but a subsystem within Earth's ecosystem, and, therefore, that ecosystem establishes the biophysical parameters of economic growth. Second, that very ecosystem is already under stress due to the economic activity of human beings.

Given these realities, those of us living in the consumerist economies of the developed world are faced with three alternative conclusions. We can have faith in the assumption that the world's economies can continue to grow indefinitely and that the world's poor will be able to have prosperous lives and a high standard of living. We can conclude that the world's poor will not, cannot, or should not attain lifestyles and will, can, or should remain poor. Or, we can conclude that alternative economic institutions must be created to meet world demand without further destroying the biosphere. Unless a model of business can be created that allows significant economic activity without further depletion of the biosphere's ability to support both life and the very economic activity on which it depends, humans are facing a global ecological, economic, and ethical tragedy.

Fortunately, some early versions of such a model of business are beginning to appear. What has been called, alternatively, "sustainable business," "the next industrial revolution," or "natural capitalism" provides models for business that can, in the words of the U.N. Commission on Sustainability, "meet the needs of the present without jeopardizing the ability of future generations to meet their own." It is a new business model that emerges out of a paradigm shift in economics, management, and ethics. We must abandon the economic model that takes unguided *growth* as the economic goal and replace it with one that targets economic *development*. Business institutions must follow this lead to find ways to meet the real needs of the world's populations without jeopardizing the biosphere's ability to meet the needs of future generations. This book surveys many of the ethical issues that will accompany the shift to a sustainable business model.

If we truly are at the very beginning of the next industrial revolution, perhaps this text is no more than a "first-draft." My deepest hope is that this book will serve to introduce students to that future and that they will quickly advance beyond what they find here.

OVERVIEW

The first six chapters of this book examine the more theoretical and philosophical aspects of sustainable business. Chapter One provides the preliminary case for a shift to sustainable business models. Chapter Two offers a glimpse of the present state of the Earth's ecology, highlighting those areas that pose the most significant challenges to environmental sustainability. Chapter Three describes the dominant economic paradigm of growth and free markets, the major alternative to sustainable business, and spells out the models of corporate social responsibility that follow from that paradigm. Chapter Four provides a detailed critique of this dominant paradigm, and defends a more active role for business institutions in addressing these challenges. Chapter Five presents the alternative economic model of sustainable economics, and sketches an alternative understanding of corporate social responsibility. Chapter Six make the business case for the shift to sustainability and provides descriptions of several conceptual frameworks that can guide the evolution of sustainable businesses.

The remaining three chapters move the focus to the more practical and managerial side of corporate sustainability. The primary purpose in these chapters remains to provide an ethical framework for sustainable business. Nonetheless, I will also try to indicate several practical developments that already are contributing to the emergence of sustainable business. Chapter Seven examines the question of sustainable production, investigating both the products themselves and the entire production process from the perspective of sustainability. Chapter Eight examines the issue of consumerism and considers business's responsibilities for hindering or encouraging sustainable consumption. Chapter Nine offers some thoughts concerning new directions that can be expected in the evolution of sustainable business. Major business professions and the functional areas within business are already beginning to address sustainability issues within their own domain. Furthermore, business's role in creating sustainable communities adds a social dimension that is often overlooked in standard discussions of business ethics.

Joseph R. DesJardins
College of St. Benedict/St. John's University

Acknowledgments

My greatest debts are to those practitioners and scholars who are at the front lines of the transformation into a sustainable economy. This textbook is a tribute to their work. I have tried to acknowledge their creativity and insights throughout this text, but if I have missed anyone I hope this general acknowledgment will suffice.

Early versions of sections of this book have been presented in various formats during the past decade. I began to develop the case for sustainable business and the critique of the dominant paradigm, essentially versions of Chapters One, Three, and Four, in the following: "Corporate Environmental Responsibility," *Journal of Business Ethics* (Vol. 17, June 1998); "Business' Environmental Responsibility" Chapter 23 of *Blackwell's Companion to Business Ethics*, Robert Frederick, ed., (Blackwell Publishing, Oxford, 1999); "Business Ethics and the Environment," chapter in *Blackwell's Guide to Business Ethics*, Norman Bowie, ed., (Blackwell Publishing, 2001). Some of the material from Chapters One and Eight appeared in "Business and Environmental Sustainability" *Business and Professional Ethics Journal* (Vol. 24, Nos. 1 & 2, 2005). I wish to acknowledge and thank the editors, reviewers, and publishers involved for their advice and encouragement. Abridged and early versions of the case for sustainable business also appeared as Chapter 9 of my *Introduction to Business Ethics* (New York: McGraw-Hill, 2005) and as "Sustainable Business" in *Contemporary Issues in Business Ethics*, 5e, edited with John McCall (Belmont, CA: Wadsworth Publishing, 2005).

Some of this material was also presented at the following: European Business Ethics Network meeting at the University of Edinburgh, Society for Business Ethics Annual Meeting, Vincentian Conference on business ethics at DePaul University, Washington and Lee University, The University of Redlands, and the University of Minnesota. I thank the conference organizers, commentators, and participants for helpful comments and advice.

I would like to acknowledge a number of individuals who shared their ideas, advice, and suggestions on various parts of this text. I owe a great debt to my friend and colleague Ernie Diedrich. Ernie and I have team-taught a class titled "Ethics and Economics of Sustainable Societies" on many occasions over the past decade. It was in this class, and owing much to Ernie's vast knowledge and enthusiasm for these topics, that I first started thinking about ethics and sustainable business. I should also thank Herman Daly and Juliet Shor, each of whom was kind enough to visit our class while they were at St. John's to deliver the annual Clemens lecture on economics. In ways that should be clear in this text, I have been greatly influenced by their work. I also thank the following individuals who offered advice and comments on written and delivered versions of this work: Bob Frederick, Norm Bowie, Ron Duska, Denis Arnold, Greg Cooper, and Jeffrey Smith.

The College of St. Benedict and St. John's University have been generous in their support. Much of this book was written while I was on a sabbatical leave, and much else was supported with faculty development funding. Finally, I would like to thank the reviewers Raymond Benton, Jr. (University of Chicago), Andrew Hoffmann (University of Michigan), Tom Eggert (University of Wisconsin-Madison), Jeffery Smith (University of Redlands), the series editor Michael Boylan and the Prentice Hall editorial and production folks.

Joseph R. DesJardins
College of St. Benedict/St. John's University

Business, Ethics, and the Environment

chapter one

The Coming Age of Sustainable Business

INTRODUCTION

This book is about what some have called "the next industrial revolution."[1] Now, at the beginning of the twenty-first century, humanity is faced with a cluster of significant economic, ecological, and ethical challenges. For billions of people, getting just the basic necessities of life—clean water, nutritious food, shelter, health care, education, jobs—is a daily struggle. Extreme poverty, exacerbated by a cycle of political repression, war, famine, and disease, is a daily fact of life across the globe. Population growth guarantees that these problems will only intensify in the immediate future. All of this is occurring at a time of unprecedented globalization. An increasingly integrated global economy means that such challenges and problems anywhere in the world will directly influence those living elsewhere.

Justice and common decency, as well as self-interest, requires that these problems be addressed by those living in the economically developed world. Addressing these challenges will require significant global economic activity, integrated with social and political leadership. However, the earth's biosphere, ultimately the only source for all this economic activity, is already under severe threat from just the type of economic growth that many assume will be the solution to these challenges.

Such factors require that business in the twenty-first century be practiced in a way that is *economically* vibrant enough to address the real needs of billions of people, yet *ecologically* informed so that the earth's capacity to support life is not diminished by that activity, and *ethically* sensitive enough that human dignity is not lost or violated in the process. Economics, ecology, and ethics form the three pillars of a sustainable society.

For some observers, these considerations suggest a "doom and gloom," pessimistic outlook. Human economic activity is straining the ability of the earth's biosphere to support the six billion people who populate the earth. I do not want to underestimate the real and significant ecological dangers we face. Nonetheless, this is also the time to call forth human creativity, imagination, and ingenuity. Although much of what I say in this book can be taken as criticism of business, and particularly of the way many businesses have operated

1

in the past, it should also be understood as a call for entrepreneurs to imagine the future and help create the sustainable business firm of the twenty-first century. Standing at the dawn of the first industrial revolution, one would have been in a similar situation. From the point of view of the old economic practices and institutions, many practitioners would have felt disparaged and under attack. But for those who were able to envision the future, the dawn of the industrial revolution was all about opportunity, potential, and hope. I believe we stand at a similar threshold in the opening years of the twentieth century.

In many practical ways, the shift to a new business and economic paradigm is already well underway. The next industrial revolution has already begun. But theory, especially concerning management ethics and corporate social responsibility, lags behind practice. Our old models of corporate social responsibility, too often grounded in the assumed value of economic growth, must be re-thought. The conventional wisdom of twentieth century business and economics must give way to a new business paradigm for the twenty-first century.

One crucial observation that will be emphasized throughout this book is that we should not underestimate the range of managerial discretion. All too often, ethical considerations have been thought of as burdens on business decision-making. But, we must recognize that business managers, rightfully, enjoy a wide range of decision-making discretion. There are many ways to pursue and attain profitability. Society must move away from the view of environmental responsibilities as side-constraints on "the" pursuit of profit, as if there is only one way to pursue profits, and ethical responsibilities are a barrier to that. Rather, we must recognize that some avenues to profitability are environmentally, and ethically, risky; other avenues are environmentally and ethically prudent and sensible. Sustainable societies generate both new responsibilities and new opportunities for business in the twenty-first century.

Both history and ethics can encourage us to think of sustainability and business in terms of conflicting worldviews and as a zero-sum game: environmentally sustainable decisions come at a cost of profitability; pursuing profits requires business managers to forgo environmental responsibility. Thus, environmental concerns must be expressed through laws that force business to do what it otherwise would not. Historically, most early environmental legislation followed the regulation-and-compliance model. Government passes laws that restrict business's freedom, and business is forced to comply with such regulation.

This regulation and compliance framework mirrors a long tradition in ethics that assumes that ethical responsibilities conflict with self-interest. To be ethical, one must forgo self-interest; if one is pursuing self-interest, one is less than ethically praiseworthy. But the possibility exists that what is right in terms of sustainability may also be right in terms of business performance. One aspect of the three pillars of sustainability, after all, is economic sustainability. If we expect business to address the significant global economic and environmental challenges of the twenty-first century, we need vibrant and stable (i.e., sustainable) businesses.

This text runs counter to the ethical tradition in which self-interest and ethical responsibility conflict. For some observers in that tradition, and perhaps especially for many in the environmental community, making "the business case" for sustainability smacks of capitulation. One should not have to prove it profitable to expect business to do the ethically right thing. Additionally, making the ethically responsible decision contingent on profits is likely to backfire when profits diminish.

But to say that sustainability is in the self-interest of business is not to say that everything that is in the interest of business is sustainable, nor is it to say that each and every business can make a profitable transition into sustainable practices. My claim is that the transition into sustainability can prove to be in the long-term interest of business's profitability and that forward-looking and entrepreneurial businesses are the ones most likely to survive into that future.

A major thesis of this book, however, is that the reigning paradigm of business and economics is incapable of adequately addressing these challenges. Conventional wisdom about economics and business involves two significantly misguided assumptions. The first is that unqualified economic *growth* is the best means for addressing global poverty and the social and ecological problems that accompany it. The second assumption is that business and economics can operate independent of environmental and ethical concerns. This book will argue for an alternative model for business and economics, what I will call the "sustainability" model, which can provide better guidance for creating a world in which we can meet the needs of the present generation without jeopardizing the ability of future generations to meet their own equally valid needs.[2] Doing this will require an alternative to economic growth, and the integration of economics, ecology, and ethics.

ECONOMICS, ECOLOGY, ETHICS

Economics. Ecology. Ethics. At first glance these fields seem unconnected. It is fair to say that in higher education, as in life, they are usually treated as distinct and independent disciplines. The standard academic paradigm places economics in the social sciences, ecology in the natural sciences, ethics in the humanities. But these words refer not only to academic disciplines, they also refer to areas of human experience. Considered from this perspective, their separation is less obvious. Economics is concerned with the ways in which human beings produce and distribute the goods and services that they need and desire. Ecology is concerned with the relationships by which humans (and other living beings) interact with their natural environment. Ethics is concerned with the basic question of how humans ought to live their lives.

The etymologic roots of the words "economics" and "ecology" reinforce this closer connection. The suffix "eco" is derived from the Greek word *oikos*, meaning household. *Nomos* is the Greek word for rules, and *logos* is the Greek word meaning an underlying principle or explanation. Thus, "eco-nomos" refers to the rules of the household; "eco-logos" refers to the underlying principles explaining the household. "Ethics" is also derived from a Greek word, *ethos*, which refers to the customs, practices, and rules by which humans live their lives. Thus, from their roots in classical Greek, economics, ecology, and ethics are all concerned with how we do and ought to manage our daily lives. As it was for the ancient Greeks, so it is also for humans of the twenty-first century, although we do not always recognize this fact.

This book argues that the integration of economics, ecology, and ethics must be a part of any legitimate attempt to address the most profound challenges of the twenty-first century. Conventional economic wisdom treats these areas as distinct, and this has had profound negative consequences for all humanity. This economic paradigm, in turn, quite literally shapes the way much of the world does business. This book will argue for an alternative model for business that seeks to integrate economic, ecological, and ethical dimensions.

Although the separation of economics from both ethics and ecology has been especially true in the industrialized societies of Europe and North America, it is fair to say that this separation is no longer simply a western prejudice. As global economies become even more integrated, western models of business and economics have been among the exports. As these western business models become truly global business models, it is crucial that we examine the assumptions of that model.

The separation of economics from ethics has not always been the case, however. Economists from Adam Smith and John Stuart Mill to Milton Friedman and Paul Krugman are known as much for the social and political views as they have for their economic research. As economics emerged as a social science in the eighteenth and nineteenth centuries, economic questions were motivated by the desire to serve the greater social good. Nevertheless, the reigning paradigm of the early twenty-first century is that economics is, and should be, value-neutral. This view is descriptively and normatively mistaken. That is, it is wrong both as a matter of fact and wrong as a matter of values. A more adequate model—both factually and ethically more adequate—must recognize that economic, ecological, and ethical concerns are all directed at the same question: What are the best ways for human beings to live and flourish within the biosphere that is their only home?

The implications of such a shift for business are substantial. If economic growth is the primary goal of the economic system in which business operates, the social responsibilities of business are fairly narrow. Business ought to pursue profit within the law and within certain minimal moral constraints. Thus, the primary, and some would say only, social responsibility of business is economic, with legal and ethical considerations functioning as side-constraints upon this primary goal. Acting in this way is thought to ensure that business activity furthers the overall social goal of economic growth, while respecting other social goals that are reflected in the law. But if this economic model is replaced by one that is attuned to ecological factors, the social responsibilities of business shift substantially. In this new model, corporate social responsibility must be assessed on three criteria: economic, ecological, and ethical. These criteria are commonly referred to as the "triple bottom line" or the "three pillars of sustainability."[3]

INDIVIDUALS, GOVERNMENT, AND BUSINESS

Another distinction that plays a role in the dominant paradigm concerns the separation of individual morality from questions of social, institutional, and political practice. From this perspective, individuals are afforded two opportunities to shape the direction of business: as citizens, individuals can demand laws requiring business to act in certain ways; as consumers they can express their demands within the marketplace. In this view, the beliefs, attitudes, desires, and values of individuals are taken as given, leaving business and government with only the relatively passive role of responding to those demands. Individuals are free to pursue their self-interest—typically understood as whatever they happen to want or desire at any particular moment—little influenced by social realities. The idea that both business and government help create and shape those beliefs, attitudes, desires, and values is seldom acknowledged. A more adequate model of sustainable business must recognize the complex web of connections between government, business, and individuals.

The uncritical trust in economic growth, the mistaken separation of economics from ecology and ethics, and the artificial separation of individuals from institutions and government are part of this dominant political and economic paradigm. Rather than discuss this paradigm in the abstract, an example will help demonstrate how this worldview translates into practical political, economic, and business policy. This example can be found in the proposed energy policy for the George W. Bush administration.

In May 2001, at the very start of the twenty-first century, Vice President of the United States Richard Cheney gave a major speech outlining the administration's energy policy. The Vice President suggested that to meet projected consumer demand, government programs must be aimed at significantly increasing the supply of fossil-fuel and nuclear-based energy. In a passage that drew wide criticism at the time, the Vice President acknowledged that "the aim here is efficiency, not austerity," concluding that "Conservation may be a sign of personal virtue, but it is not a sufficient basis for a sound, comprehensive energy policy."[4]

The speech emphasized the supply side of energy policy, focusing on building new fossil-fuel and nuclear-power plants and the infrastructure to transport that power. For the most part, the speech disregarded conservation and alternative energy sources. The view here is clear. Although individual citizens are free to choose to conserve resources, government has no role in promoting that choice. Rational public policy should assume that consumers will not choose to conserve. Therefore, public policy should prepare to meet an ever-growing demand for energy resources, a demand best met by increasing the supply of the already dominant energy sources.

This speech was notable for many reasons, not the least of which is that it found a conservative Republican administration down-playing the personal virtue of conservation while promoting massive government intervention in economic markets. These policies would have had the U.S. Federal government providing huge subsidies and tax incentives for some businesses (e.g., in the oil, coal, and nuclear industries) and thereby creating enormous barriers to entry for other businesses (e.g., in the alternative energy sector). For an administration that widely advocated free market policies, this proposal was a striking example of centralized government planning and interference in the market. Consumers may well be demanding more energy, but this proposal had government choosing to subsidize fossil fuels and nuclear power as the preferable means for meeting that demand.

Perhaps more interesting than the speech's political implications was the almost total disregard for the role of business in matters of national energy use and energy policy. Individuals were seen as free to choose to conserve, or not. Government's role is to ensure an adequate energy supply to meet the inevitably growing demand efficiently. Left unsaid was the role of business. The implicit view is that individual consumers and government are the active players in energy policy while business remains as a relatively passive spectator. Business responds to the demands of consumers, and obeys the laws passed by government. Business was not expected, nor asked, to take a leadership role in developing future energy policy other than, presumably, to lobby for its own self-interests.

However, the connection between the personal domain of individuals, the institutional domain of business, and the political domain of government is enormously more complex than is suggested by this reigning paradigm. Individuals are not only consumers, they are also citizens. Government not only reacts to the demands of its citizens, it also shapes and directs the attitudes, beliefs, and values of those citizens. Government not only regulates business, it promotes, directs, and, for better or worse, serves business interests. Similarly, business not only responds to consumer demand, it also helps create and shape that demand through advertising and marketing. Business not only responds to government policy, it also helps create and shape that policy.

A comprehensive approach to the social and environmental responsibilities of business must recognize this complexity. Individuals act as both citizens and consumers, pursuing both their best interests and their consumer desires, able to act both selfishly and for the common good. What consumers demand in the marketplace depends on what is available in the marketplace, what they know about, and at what cost. Government policies that provide tax incentives for coal-fired power plants, which allow oil exploration on public land, which provide massive military protection for foreign oil fields, or which limit legal liability for nuclear power plants, give those industries a competitive advantage in the marketplace. This advantage increases the relative price of alternative energy sources and thereby determines what consumers are free to demand in that market. Because government cannot avoid influencing public opinion, it has a responsibility to respond to public opinion and to guide it. Political leaders not only respond to the demands of citizens, they unavoidably guide and direct those demands. Likewise, business has responsibilities to respond to the demands of the marketplace and to lead markets to a better future. Creative, entrepreneurial business leaders not only react to consumer demand, they also create, shape, and influence those markets. The history of the consumer electronic industry from personal computers to the iPod, and the vast amounts spent on marketing and advertising by contemporary business, testify to this reality.

ECONOMIC GROWTH: PROBLEM OR SOLUTION?

The Vice President's speech also exemplified the reigning paradigm in its unquestioned allegiance to the idea that "sound and comprehensive" social policy should be based on economic growth. The challenge for policy makers, according to Cheney, is to bring supply more in line with demand. "As a country, we have demanded more and more energy but we have not brought on-line the supplies needed to meet that demand. . . . In the next two decades, the country's demand for oil will grow by a third, yet we are producing less oil today—39 percent less than we were in 1970. . . . By 2020, our demand [for natural gas] will increase by two-thirds. An overall demand for electric power is expected to rise by 43 percent over the next 20 years." The solution? "Over the next 20 years, just meeting projected demand will require between 1300 and 1900 new power plants . . . That averages out to more than one new power plant per week every week for the next 20 years."

The standard model of economic and social policy treats consumer demand as a given. Neither economics nor government has any role in assessing either the quantity (that consumers might be demanding too much) or quality (that they might be demanding the wrong things) of consumer demand. How much consumers demand and what, in fact, they demand, is beyond the pale of economic, political, or ethical assessment. Given this starting point, economic growth is the only available policy option. "Sound and comprehensive" public policy must assume an unending growth in consumer demand and that satisfying that demand is a good thing. The challenge for business and government is to find ways to meet that growing demand. Extended globally, this model treats economic growth as the solution for all problems. A bigger economy is a better economy.

However, there are good reasons for thinking that economic growth alone cannot be a long-term solution to the challenges of poverty and ecological destruction. Later chapters will review the case against economic growth on environmental and ethical grounds in more detail. But for now, a brief example can raise this issue clearly. Consider the ecological implications if the approach presented by the Vice President had been extended just within the United States from the date he delivered this speech. By 2007, there would have been six new fossil-fuel or nuclear power plants in each state. Extend this vision, and add one additional power plant being built in each state every year for the indefinite future. Imagine the infrastructure, the train lines, power lines, the mines and oil fields, highways, and oil tankers that would already be necessary to support such growth. Imagine the greenhouse gases emitted into the atmosphere as a result. Imagine the amount of nuclear waste generated if, as the Vice President argued, nuclear power plants are made a part of the mix. Imagine how the decisions would be made for locating such socially undesirable building projects.

Now, consider extending this model internationally, as the world's economies become even more integrated. Can you imagine a similar energy strategy in China with its population of 1.6 billion people, five times the population of the United States? Could this model be extended also to include India with its population of 1 billion people, and expanded to an additional 1 billion people in Indonesia, Brazil, Russia, Pakistan, Bangladesh, and Nigeria?

The Vice-President's speech highlighted the assumptions of the reigning economic and political paradigm. That paradigm assumes that unguided economic growth can, will, and should go on indefinitely. It assumes that consumers will continue to demand a greater amount of the types of products they already use. It assumes that the primary responsibility of business and government is to respond to consumer demand so conceived. It assumes that economic growth is both ecologically and ethically benign, if not positive.

In light of such factors, citizens and businesses in developed western economies are faced with three options—either (1) we share the faith that economic growth and consumerism can be extended throughout the entire world, that global economies can grow indefinitely, and that unregulated growth will, "as if guided by an invisible hand," adequately address poverty and ecological destruction; or, (2) we believe that developing economies somehow cannot, will not, or should not, attain the economic and consumer lifestyle similar to that found in the industrialized world; or (3) we help create a new paradigm in which the economic well-being of the entire world's population does not threaten ecological stability. I suggest that neither of the first two options is defensible or plausible. We need to develop a new paradigm for a sustainable economy and sustainable business.

THE SUSTAINABILITY PARADIGM

Like the first industrial revolution of the eighteenth and nineteenth centuries, the new industrial revolution will grow out of, and have implications for, our personal, social, cultural, business, economic, and political life. That first revolution, originating primarily in Western Europe and the United States, was greatly helped by scientific advances in physics, chemistry, and biology, and technological advances in bringing power-driven machinery to transportation, manufacturing, and agriculture. That revolution was also accelerated by social, ecological, and economic factors. Increased populations, and increased mobility of those populations, provided cheap and plentiful workers for factories, and consumers for products. The oak forests that once covered much of the northern European countryside had been decimated for farmland, fuel, and timber, creating both an incentive and an opportunity for coal power and imported timber and manufactured materials. Famine, caused by both political repression and crop failures, also helped depopulate some countryside and create large pools of emigrants to supply cheap labor for foreign factories. Wars created incentives for new technologies that soon translated for commercial purposes and, once ended, supplied even more cheap labor for industry. Advances in transportation, primarily rail and shipping, created unprecedented global economic connections.

Similar factors suggest the possibility for a new emerging revolution. Scientific and technological advances in transportation, energy, biotechnology, and electronics provide significant resources for global economic development. Globalization, and all that this implies for culture, politics, and economics, suggests that we are at another historical turning point. Indeed, we may already be living in the age of global economic integration, an age captured in journalist Thomas Friedman's phrase that "the earth is flat." Poverty, population growth, especially in the world's poorest regions, and worldwide ecological threats, provide us with the motivation to create a more just and environmentally sound economic model. Part of this new reality is captured in the common phrase: "poverty anywhere is a threat to prosperity everywhere."

The concept of sustainability has grown out of the recognition that economic development on a global level cannot be separated from questions of social justice and from ecological stability. The new worldview emerging as an alternative to the reigning paradigm of economic growth and free markets holds that long-term sustainability is the criterion of successful economic and social development. Sustainability, in this sense, is understood to involve three dimensions: economic, ecological, and ethical. Following common usage, I refer to these as the *three pillars of sustainability*. Business, within this conceptualization, is no longer understood as having a primary economic goal, with ethical and environmental consideration functioning as side-constraints. Business has three equally compelling goals that must be balanced over the long-term.

Claiming that economic growth is part of the problem is not to envision a future of economic depression or stagnation. Without significant economic activity, human suffering will get worse not better. Nor is it to imagine the creation of romantic, bucolic agricultural communities. There are 10 urban areas in the world with populations greater than 15 million, and another 15 with populations greater than 10 million. The people living in each of these urban areas are not likely to voluntarily emigrate out into the countryside to start peaceful agricultural communes. There are reasons, after all, that populations have emigrated from the countryside into urban centers. Economic growth itself is not bad—some things will need to grow to address these challenges. Unqualified and undirected economic growth is the problem.

The alternative to economic growth is economic development, not economic stagnation. Following the economist Herman Daly, we should distinguish between economic "growth" and economic "development."[5] Growth means getting bigger; development means getting better. Not all growth is good, as our knowledge of cancer would demonstrate. Likewise, not all economic activity is good. Standard models of economic growth, the gross domestic product (GDP) for example, treat any economic activity as a good thing. On this model, money spent cleaning up after an environmental disaster is a good thing. Buying a $60 thousand SUV contributes more to the economy, and, therefore, to society, than purchasing a $20 thousand hybrid car. Bulldozing a pristine woodland and building tract homes and strip malls is the type of economic "development" government should encourage. But true economic *development* must encourage targeted economic growth in those areas in which human well-being can be promoted in ecologically sustainable ways and a decrease of those economic activities that degrade the earth's biosphere.

The economic growth paradigm has direct implications for the social responsibility of business. In a later chapter, I will argue against standard models of corporate social responsibility, which presume the ethical legitimacy of uncritical economic growth. I will argue that the social responsibility of business must be assessed not only in economic and ethical terms, but also in ecological ones. The sustainability model for economics and business is challenged to provide an alternative to this growth-is-all mentality.

SUSTAINABILITY AS SOCIAL JUSTICE

In later sections, a variety of specific ethical considerations that support the movement toward sustainability are considered in more depth. In particular, Chapter Six will make the "business case" for sustainability, arguing that there are strong self-interested reasons for business to adopt more sustainable practices. Chapter Two will also review a range of values that support the protection and preservation of the global biosphere. As a background for these discussions, it will be helpful to begin with some more general reflections on sustainability and social justice.

As defined in the Brundtland Commission in 1987, the very concept of sustainable development involves a social justice component. The definition describes sustainable development as "development that meets the needs of the present without compromising the ability of future generations to meet their own needs." At first glance, this definition includes several core features of justice, including considerations of equal opportunity, liberty, and fairness.

In general, this definition of sustainability can be thought of as providing an answer to the basic question of distributive justice: On what grounds should goods and resources be allocated? The sustainability answer is given in terms that are familiar to any theory of justice. Goods and resources ought to be distributed in ways that meet the needs of the present generation without denying future generations an equal opportunity to meet their own needs.

Discussions of distributive justice often begin with Aristotle's understanding of justice as treating equals equally and thus giving each person his or her due. This is a formal definition in that what each person is due is unspecified. It also does not explain which inequalities would justify unequal shares of which specific goods and resources. Examining these questions can help us explain the sense in which social justice commits one to sustainability.

When applied to the Brundtland definition, treating equals equally might suggest that future generations have a right to the same goods and resources available to the present generation. For some goods that are not depleted when used—such as solar energy or economic services—the present use of these resources does not restrict future use and thus can be justly used without concern for future needs. But other goods and resources raise problems for an egalitarian conception of distributive justice.

Consider the example of nonrenewable resources. A strict egalitarian theory of distributive justice would hold that every generation has a right to an equal amount of the resources. But, by definition, any use of nonrenewable resources will result in less of it available for future use. Thus, it might appear that any use of nonrenewable resources would be unjust to future people. However, if this is true for the present generation, it would be equally true for any future generation. This implies that no one has a right to use any nonrenewable resource.

This problem leads many to support a conception of justice as equal opportunity or equal consideration, rather than as equality of results or goods. This understanding also is more compatible with the Brundtland definition, which emphasizes the equal ability to meet one's needs rather equality of resources themselves. Egalitarian justice requires not that future generations have the same resources available to them, but that they have an equal opportunity to attain those ends for which we use those resources. Future generations have an equal right to the productive capacity of such things as soil and fossil fuels, rather than to the resources themselves.

This approach to economic justice has deep roots in the western legal and political traditions. One finds a similar conclusion in John Locke's classic defense of a natural right to private property.[6] Locke argued that one acquires an ethically legitimate claim to private ownership of property when one "mixes his labor" with what was previously unowned. Locke reasoned that each individual had a natural right over their own body and their own labor, the natural rights to life and liberty. Locke then derived a right to own and use property as a means for securing one's rights to life and liberty.

But Locke immediately recognized that this property right could infringe on the more fundamental rights of equality and liberty. The right to private ownership is derived from each individual's personal liberty to use and control one's own labor. But this means that *my* ownership of private property can be justified only if it does not violate the equal rights of other persons to use their own labor to acquire private property. Thus, Locke concluded that private ownership can be ethically justified only when "enough and as good" property remains for others. Thus, the equal rights of others are violated by my taking possession of property if those others are denied an equal opportunity to attain similar property rights.

Locke's theory is instructive because he also recognized that unowned and available property was significantly limited, and, as a result, there was not "enough and as good" remaining for all people. But, with the creation of currency, society has created a substitute for real property. As long as each individual can sell labor for wages and use those wages to buy property, their equal rights are not violated. Applying Locke's reasoning to the present, we might conclude that the private acquisition of productive resources by the present generation is ethically justified as long as future generations have an equal opportunity themselves to acquire the productive resources necessary to secure their equal rights to life and liberty.

Philosopher Brian Barry offered a similar argument in defense of the claim that we have duties to future generations.[7] Barry argued that present generations have a right to use nonrenewable resources, even if this puts future people at a relative disadvantage, as long as we compensate future generations for this loss. Although we cannot compensate them by returning the resources themselves, we can compensate by ensuring that they have an equal opportunity to those goods produced by those resources. Humans value such resources as oil and coal not as ends in themselves, but as means to secure other central human interests. Future generations have an ethical claim upon us, not to preserve resources *per se*, but to preserve their equal ability to meet their own needs.

The conception of justice implicit with the sustainability paradigm commits us to respecting equal opportunity rights of both geographically and temporally distant people. The rights of the world's poor as well as the rights of future generations to attain appropriate natural resources and use them for their own needs are no more, and no less, ethically important than our own. When our actions deny others this equal opportunity, we have an obligation to compensate them for this loss. We can fulfill this obligation not only by preserving the resources themselves, but by ensuring that other people have an equal opportunity to the productive capacity of those resources.

In practical terms, this suggests our duty to invest in the technology that will be needed for future people to maintain equal opportunities. It suggests a duty to invest in research and development to produce alternatives to our use of nonrenewable resources. We should use renewable resources only at rates at which they can be renewed. We have a duty to conserve and not waste resources. Most generally, we have a duty to give them equal consideration in our deliberations about what we should do, and how we should act.

Two final considerations are worth mentioning in regard to the justice of sustainability. First, although this discussion has been presented in terms of rights and duties, similar conclusions would be reached by relying on a more utilitarian ethic. Any plausible interpretation of the utilitarian principle to maximize the overall good requires sustaining the productive capacity of the earth's biosphere to meet the needs of present and future generations. Just as sound advice for one's long-term financial well-being is to live off of interest rather than savings, preserving the productive capacity of natural resources contributes to long-term happiness.

Finally, it is worth pointing to the use of the language of "needs" in the Brundtland definition of sustainability. This suggests a ranking of the ends toward which humans act, distinguishing mere desires from needs. Philosophers use a number of concepts to express this idea: primary goods, basic goods, central interests. The point is that not all things that we want or desire deserve to be attained, and when there is a conflict between needs and wants, needs have an ethical priority. The language of rights is often used to make this point. I may desire and want many things, but I can claim a right only to those basic goods, or central interests that are identified as needs. The justice associated with sustainability is concerned with protecting and preserving needs, not merely desires. By implication, when the desires of present generations conflict with the needs of future generations, the needs trump the desires.

Sustainability: Two Caveats

Before turning to a closer look at sustainable business, it is worthwhile to issue two *caveats* concerning the very notion of sustainability. First, although the concept of sustainability can offer a pragmatic guide for future business directions, it must not be so broadly conceived that just any practice or any business can become sustainable. When we hear talk about "sustainability," we should always be prepared to ask "*What* is being sustained?" "*For whom* is it being sustained?" "*How* is it being sustained?" and "What *should* be sustained?"

The language of sustainability has proven quite popular, even among those who otherwise might not be identified as environmentalists. This should give us pause. It seems clear that sustainability is often assumed to mean "sustaining present business patterns and present levels of consumption." In this way, defending a model of sustainable development would mean simply sustaining the status quo. Some have even spoken of "sustainable growth" which, as Herman Daly argues, is impossible. To the degree that present consumption patterns, particularly those found in consumer-driven industrial economies, are causing environmental deterioration, the status quo is exactly what we need to change. To the degree that certain products or industries are destroying the biosphere's ability to support life, they will need to change. To the degree that a maldistribution of the world's resources results in extreme poverty for billions of people, the status quo will need to change. The type of economic growth that characterizes present economic models is not sustainable. Make no mistake, sustainable living and sustainable development will require a changed economy and changed culture within the consumerist societies of the industrialized world. There may well be industries and social practices that are incompatible with sustainable development. Sustainability will also require substantial closure of the economic gap between wealthy industrialized countries and the poor developing world. We need to be vigilant and not use sustainable development simply as a fashionable way to talk about continued economic growth, consumption, or industrialism.

Second, the concept of "sustainability" most accurately applies only at more general and systemic levels. An individual firm, for example, may adopt the most ecologically benign and safe practices, but if the economic system or biosphere in which it is embedded collapses, the firm itself will not be sustained. On the other hand, an ecologically destructive practice, such as the creation of nuclear wastes or the destruction of a wetland, can be sustained as long as it occurs as an isolated incident within an otherwise healthy biosphere. An individual business or a particular practice is neither sustainable nor unsustainable in isolation of wider economic and ecological systems. "Sustainability" truly applies only to practices that have an impact, positive or negative, on the broader biosphere. Nevertheless, for convenience sake, we can talk about a sustainable business as a shorthand way of describing practices that, if generalized over an industry or economy, would make positive contributions to long-term economic, ecological, and ethical sustainability.

But before turning to the ethics and economics of sustainable business, it will be worthwhile to provide a brief review of the economic, ecological, and ethical challenges facing human beings in the first decades of the twenty-first century.

Endnotes

1 See, for example, William McDonough and Michael Braungart, "The Next Industrial Revolution" *The Atlantic Monthly* (Oct. 1998), vol. 282, No. 4, pp. 88–92.

2 Perhaps the most widely used definition of sustainability comes from the United Nations' Brundtland Commission. The Brundtland Commission published its findings on economic development and the environment in 1987 in a book titled *Our Common Future*. This book offered what has become the standard definition of sustainable development: "sustainable development is development that meets the needs of the present without compromising the ability of future generations to meet their own needs."

3 The "triple bottom line" framework is presented in most detail by John Elkington in *Cannibals With Forks The Triple Bottom Line of the 21st Century Business* New Society Publishers (Gabriola, BC, 1998). The "three pillars" image is often traced to the Bruntland Commission's explicit integration of economics, ecology, and ethics.

4 Vice President Richard Cheney, speech to the Associated Press annual meeting, Toronto. May 5, 2001.

5 Herman Daly, "Sustainable Growth: An Impossibility Theorem," reprinted in *Valuing the Earth*, ed. Herman Daly and Kenneth Townsend (Boston: Massachusetts Institute of Technology Press, 1987), pp. 267–268.

6 John Locke, *Second Treatise on Government*, ed. C.B. Macpherson (Indianapolis, IN: Hackett Publishing, 1980), see especially Chapter 5.

7 Brian Barry, "Intergenerational Justice in Energy Policy," in McLean and Brown, eds., *Energy and the Future* (Totawa, NJ: Rowman and Littlefield, 1983), pp. 15–30.

chapter two

The Biosphere: Facts and Values

INTRODUCTION

The earth's biosphere is the thin band surrounding the surface of the earth in which life can survive. Life has been found surrounding hot vents in the deepest ocean trenches and on barren mountaintops. The deepest ocean trench is 6.75 miles deep, and the highest mountain is 5.5 miles above sea level. This means that the entire biosphere, the area in which all life on earth might exist, is less than 13 miles wide. In practical terms, the area in which life can survive is much narrower, and for human life narrower still. In fact, human life can thrive within less than the 2-mile band extending approximately from sea level to an elevation of perhaps 10,000 feet. Roughly 70 percent of that surface area is covered by oceans. Although oceans are essential to sustain life, humans themselves can live only on the remaining 30 percent of the earth's surface. Of that, many regions are inhospitable for human habitation as being too dry, too cold, too barren, and too mountainous. Although human life can exist only within narrow areas of the biosphere, it nonetheless requires much else to survive. The earth's atmosphere blocks some harmful solar radiation from reaching us while allowing just enough radiation in which to maintain a livable range of temperatures. The oceans also play a pivotal and complex role in maintaining a climate that is hospitable to humans and providing essential food and water.

By some measures, the remaining land area is sufficient to meet human needs. As anyone who has flown in an airplane realizes, much of the earth's land mass appears empty of human habitation. The oceans and the earth itself contain seemingly immeasurable resources to support life. However, by other measures this biosphere is very fragile indeed. Slight changes in temperature, rainfall, atmosphere, sunlight, soil fertility, ocean currents, or ocean levels would dramatically change Earth's ability to support life. As a context for our examination of sustainable business, in this chapter we review some of the ecological challenges that face the biosphere over the coming decades and some reasons that humans ought to value it. What are the facts, and why should anyone care?

I = PAT

During the 1970s, some of the earliest debates within the environmental movement concerned the relative significance of population and technology as primary causes of environmental harm. One side, for which Paul Ehrlich was the best-known advocate, argued that population growth had the greatest impact on the environment. The other side, represented most notably by Barry Commoner, argued that technology, and the consumerist lifestyle of industrial society, had the greater impact. Emerging from these debates was a formula that is now widely used in thinking about environmental impact: $I = PAT$. Environmental impact (I) is a product of population (P), consumption per capita, or affluence (A), and technology (T).

The insight expressed by the formula is reasonably clear. The three major variables that explain environmental impact are population size, consumption patterns, and technology. If we hold consumption patterns and technology constant, a larger population will have a greater environmental impact than a smaller one. If we hold population and technology constant, a society that consumes more per capita will have a greater environmental impact than one consuming less. If we hold population and consumption constant, a highly industrialized society will have a greater environmental impact than a less industrialized one. A sustainable world would balance population, consumption, and technology in such a way that the overall environmental impact is benign.

The exact meaning and appropriate use of this formula is contentious, as would be expected of any attempt to capture complex relationships in a simple formula. Nevertheless, it can be usefully employed as a model for thinking about the relationship between environmental problems and their underlying causal factors. Importantly, for this book, we should also note that each of the three variables can have a negative value. That is, some consumption patterns and some technologies, like population declines, can reverse or lessen harmful environmental impacts.

This model also can be helpful for thinking about where business fits into these issues. Although population control seems beyond the responsibility of business, both consumption patterns and technology are clearly business concerns. Decisions made within businesses influence, positively or negatively, both consumption per capita (A), and technology (T). Business decisions can, therefore, both increase and decrease the overall environmental impact of any given society. In many ways, this entire book is about business' responsibility for A and T. Some business activities and technologies have an overall negative environmental impact; others might contribute positively to environmental sustainability. Before investigating these factors in more detail, in this chapter we review the environmental impact (I) of present practices and population projections (P) for the near future.

STATE OF THE BIOSPHERE

Because the political, social, and economic implications are enormous, any attempt to describe the present state of the earth's ecological health will be controversial. This chapter can provide only a very general and cursory overview of the environmental impact of present production schemes. However, any fair assessment suggests that the Earth's biosphere is under stress, and, because all life depends on a healthy biosphere, a reasonable conclusion is that humans need to proceed cautiously. Readers are encouraged to do their own research into the present state of the biosphere.[1]

To support human life, the Earth's biosphere must provide adequate food, water, and breathable air. It must maintain a stable atmosphere and a moderate climate, and it must shelter life from solar radiation. It must provide energy to fuel all these activities, the materials out of which they will be produced, and it must be capable of absorbing the wastes produced by them. For the sake of our children, grandchildren, and all future generations, it must be capable of doing all of these things over the long term.

Food

We can usefully divide human food sources into three categories: agricultural crops, fisheries, and animal farming. Although each area has proven resilient in meeting growing demand, each also shows unambiguous signs of stress.

Historians sometimes speak of three agricultural revolutions. The first was prehistoric and occurred when humans first began establishing relatively permanent settlements in which domesticated animals and farming replaced hunting and gathering as the primary food production. The second, beginning in the late eighteenth century, was fueled by advances in crop rotation, mechanical technology, animal breeding, and land reform. The resulting great increases in productivity provided food for growing the exploding urban centers of the industrial revolution. In each of the first two agricultural revolutions, the amount of land cultivated increased significantly to account for the growth in food production. The third revolution began in the latter half of the twentieth century when chemical fertilizers increased fertility, pesticides decreased losses, industrial production methods and technology increased efficiency, and genetics created higher yielding varieties of crops. Unlike the first two revolutions, the third revolution was fueled by increasing productivity from land already under cultivation, rather than an increase in cultivated land area itself. But these recent advances are not without their costs.

In 1798, early enough in the midst of the second agricultural revolution that its effects were not yet understood, economist Thomas Malthus published "*An Essay on the Principle of Population, as it Affects the Future*

Improvement of Society." Malthus famously predicted that population, advancing geometrically, was fast outpacing the food production, which advances arithmetically. Malthus predicted that poverty, famine, disease, and conflict would inevitably result unless humans consciously took steps to control population. Malthus failed to realize that he was living in the midst of the very agricultural revolution that would falsify his predictions. Similarly, in 1972 the well-known Club of Rome report, *Limits to Growth*, predicted dire consequences if present trends in resource use, population, pollution, and industrialization continued unchanged.[2] Yet, food and materials production over the following decades not only kept pace with population but made some real gains. Some contemporary observers claim that recent predictions of environmental disaster suffer from the same mistake that Malthus made. The *Limits to Growth* analysis, like Malthus, failed to appreciate the ability of human creativity, in the form of science, technology, and entrepreneurial skills to keep food production in line with population growth. According to these observers, there is no reason to doubt that increases in productivity cannot continue indefinitely.

At about the same time that *Limits of Growth* was published, the United Nations sponsored the first World Food Conference. At that conference, world leaders committed themselves to ending hunger within a decade. In fact, significant progress was made in that hunger in the less industrialized countries was cut in half within two decades as the effects of the third agricultural revolution took hold. When the United Nations reconvened a World Food Summit in 1996, the estimated number of undernourished people worldwide was 800 million. The commitment at this summit was to reduce hunger by half within two decades. Five years later, the Summit recommitted to this same goal while acknowledging that little had changed in the intervening five years. In 2002, the UN Food and Agriculture Organization (FAO) estimated that there were 815 million undernourished people in the world in 1997 through 1999, of which 777 million were in the developing world, 27 million in the countries in transition, and 11 million in the developed market economies. The FAO acknowledged that significant progress had been made over two decades. Undernourishment in the developing countries decreased from 29 percent in 1979 to 1981 to 17 percent in 1997 to 1999, and the overall number of undernourished people had declined worldwide by 39 million since 1990.[3]

Some advances clearly have been made to address world hunger, yet signs suggest greater challenges ahead. First, we must recognize a distinction between total food availability and access to that food. Even if worldwide agricultural productivity has increased in recent decades, that food seldom reaches those most in need. Poverty prevents many who need food from getting a sufficient supply. The World Bank estimated that in 1999 1.2 billion people worldwide lived on less than $1 a day, and 2.8 billion lived on less than $2 a day.[4] Political boundaries, wars, and corruption prevent many from accessing available food. Maldistribution of food resources—too few people getting good food and too many people getting the wrong kind of food— means that the distribution of food is less than optimal. Although millions go without food, millions of others overeat high-fat and unhealthy food. The Centers for Disease Control and Prevention in the United States estimated that in 2000, 59 million Americans were obese. From 1970 to 2000, the number of obese children between the ages of 6 and 19 had doubled to 15 percent of that population. Obesity was identified as the second leading cause of avoidable death in the United States, closely rivaling tobacco as the single biggest avoidable cause of death.[5]

We must also recognize that increased productivity has been the result of three fundamental changes in agriculture: increased use of synthetic pesticides and fertilizers, increased irrigation, and genetic modification of crops. Each of these changes has significant ecological and environmental costs attached to it.

Since publication of Rachel Carson's *Silent Spring* in 1962, we have been aware of the dangers of pesticides to both human and nonhuman life. There are more than 875 active ingredients in pesticides officially registered with the Environmental Protection Agency, and these are sold as part of 21,000 separate products.[6] In the United States, more than 3 pounds of active ingredient pesticides is used every year for every person, and in the largest agricultural production state of California, the average is more than 6.5 pounds per person. These figures are only for the active ingredient, oftentimes less than 1 percent of the total weight of the pesticide compound.[7] Forty registered and legal pesticides have been known to cause cancer in animals, and have been associated with childhood leukemia, brain tumors, Hodgkin's lymphoma, and prostate cancer. Forty-three registered pesticides are known to cause birth defects or other reproductive harms, or to impair child development. Several studies found a mixture of pesticide residues in the blood and urine of almost 100 percent of all persons sampled.[8] Besides consumers, farmers and agricultural workers face particularly intensive threats from pesticide use. Because the plant, insect, and microbial life targeted by pesticides have short reproductive cycles and high reproductive rates, immunity to pesticides occurs frequently, promoting a cycle of new and more powerful pesticides. Evidence suggests that the number of crops loss to insect and weeds have actually increased since the 1940s when synthetic pesticide use was first widely introduced.[9]

More intensive irrigation has also contributed to increase agricultural productivity, but this, too, has significant costs. It has been estimated that 70 percent of all water pumped from underground aquifers or diverted from rivers is used for agriculture, 20 percent for industrial purposes, and 10 percent for residential use. Over-pumping of aquifers has reduced water tables significantly in the United States, China, India, Mexico, the Middle East, and in North Africa. Major rivers in the United States and Mexico (the Colorado River and the Rio Grande), India (the Ganges), Pakistan (Indus), and Central

Asia (Amu Dar'ya) are now dry for portions of each year. Major inland seas, most famously the Aral Sea in Central Asian and Lake Chad in Northern Africa, have dried up drastically.[10]

Genetically modified crops are the third major factor in increasing agricultural productivity. Creating plant hybrids and cross-breeding have been practiced by farmers for centuries, but modern biochemistry now enables scientists to create entirely new organisms by altering the genetic make-up of both plants and animals. Genetically modified organisms (GMOs) face widespread public opposition throughout much of the world. Opponents cite potential health risks, ecosystem damage and threats to biodiversity, the concentration of power in the hands of a few giant agribusinesses, and the commercialization of life in their criticisms of GM foods. More generally, despite its promise to increase food supply for impoverished regions, much GM research is focused on crops intended for animal feed (soybeans and corn), non-food crops (cotton), and the potential pharmaceutical uses of crops (biopharming). Although each of these uses has the potential to benefit those most in need, the benefits of these advances will more likely be used by those who already have plentiful calories, clothing, and medical care.

Finally, two emerging trends would create limits to agricultural productivity even if the challenges of pesticides, water availability, and GM crops are met. In many areas of the world, a combination of agricultural practices and natural processes are degrading the productivity of cropland and range land. Desertification, the process by which formerly productive land is degraded to the point that it no longer is productive, is occurring throughout the world and effects millions of people.[11] The U.N. Food and Agriculture Organization reports that "over 250 million people are directly affected by desertification. [and] some one thousand million (or one billion) people in over one hundred countries are at risk. These people include many of the world's poorest, most marginalized, and politically weak citizens."[12] Erosion, soil compaction, salinization (salt build-up in soils), a decline in soil fertility, a build-up of toxic substances, and water-logged soil all add to the amount of degraded and less productive croplands worldwide.

Second, increasing global temperature has the potential to play havoc with agricultural productivity. The 1990s was the warmest decade on record. Since accurate data from scientific instruments were first available in the late 1800s, the 12 warmest years on record were, in descending order, 2005, 1998, 2002, 2003, 2004, 2001, 1997, 1995, 1990, 1999, 1991, and 2000.[13] This temperature rise is almost certainly the result of a build-up of greenhouse gases, most notably carbon dioxide, in the atmosphere. If so, it is likely to continue into the indefinite future. The consequences of such global warming will vary across the globe. There would surely be some agricultural benefits of a generalized global warming: longer growing seasons and more temperate winters in some regions, higher yields of some crops, and perhaps even more rain in some areas. But there will certainly be agricultural disasters as well. In tropical and subtropical regions, many crops already are at their maximum level of heat tolerance and are already suffering from water shortages, lack of irrigation, and desertification. Regions to which warmer crops might migrate may well lack the irrigation and soil to support new crop species. Increased temperatures would also likely result in more flooding along coasts (the world's most populated geographical area) and prolonged droughts in already arid and semiarid regions.

Moving beyond agriculture, improvement in global food production in the late twentieth century was also due to increased fishing yields. However, worldwide fisheries face, if anything, even greater problems at present than agriculture. Worldwide fish catch has not increased since its peak of 86 million metric tons in 1989. In many years since, global fish catch has declined. With worldwide population increasing during this period, fish production per capita has declined by 17 percent, from 14.6 kg per person in 1987 to 13.1 kg in 2000. Since 1998, China alone has accounted for almost 20 percent of the global fish catch. Fish harvest in major areas in the Atlantic, Pacific, and Mediterranean have declined significantly. The once plentiful fisheries of Canada's Grand Banks and Georges Banks off the New England coast have essentially collapsed. Many commercial fish species, including the cod, haddock, blue-fin tuna, swordfish, red snapper, and redfish, are largely depleted. Many lakes, rivers, and ocean areas, including a large region in the Gulf of Mexico at the mouth of the Mississippi River, can barely support life as the result of oxygen depletion brought on by agricultural run-off. In 1995, the United Nation's Food and Agriculture Organization reported that "about 70 percent of the world's marine fish stocks are heavily exploited, overexploited, depleted, or slowly recovering."[14] Each of these categories identifies a fish population that is unsustainable.

Finally, animal farming is the third major area of food production. Cattle, poultry, hogs, and sheep are the four major animal groups raised for food. Increased production of animals during the last few decades has come primarily as the result of more intensive, industrial models of farming. Like crops, we have not significantly expanded the land area devoted to raising animals; we simply raise more animals per area.

There are considerable problems associated with this type of industrial animal farming. Groundwater pollution from giant feedlots and hog farms is a growing concern in every area in which such practices exist. There is widespread and global opposition to the way animals are treated (or mistreated) by animal farms, ranches, and slaughterhouses. Problems of *E. coli*, salmonella, and mad cow disease are commonly linked more to practices of large slaughterhouses and processing plants than to small farms and ranches. Range land used to graze animals, most of it in the United States subsidized by taxpayers, is threatened with overgrazing and degradation. The demand for and marketing of meat products creates incentives to use agricultural lands to grow animal feed rather than human food, resulting in an overall loss of productive efficiency. It also creates incentives to increase deforestation in developing countries where forests are turned into grazing lands.

In conclusion, the ever-increasing demand for food from a growing worldwide population confronts us with important choices. We can continue present trends and trust that the biosphere is resilient enough to overcome these problems, or we seek alternative sustainable approaches to food production.

Climate

The biggest single threat to the biosphere's ability to provide humans with a livable climate comes from global warming. Widespread public debate has focused on this issue for more than two decades. Critics have challenged the existence of the greenhouse effect, the fact of global warming, and the catastrophic predictions based on the alleged fact of global warming.

Despite these challenges, the "greenhouse effect" has been well-confirmed through observation and experiments during the past century and is now the prevailing scientific explanation of the atmosphere's role in regulating the earth's temperature. The "greenhouse effect" occurs when certain gases—primarily water vapor and carbon dioxide, along with trace amounts of ozone, methane, nitrous oxide, and chlorofluorocarbons (CFCs)—trap heat within the atmosphere, much as the glass in a greenhouse functions to allow warming sunlight in while preventing the warmer air from escaping. There is no serious scientific dispute about the reality of the greenhouse effect and the critical role of water vapor and carbon dioxide in causing this effect.

There is also no scientific dispute any longer on the fact that there is a significant increase in such greenhouse gases being emitted into the atmosphere. Measurements have demonstrated that the concentration of atmospheric carbon dioxide have increased significantly since the industrial revolution and now exist at levels unsurpassed in hundreds of thousands, if not millions, of years. Fossil fuel use in automobiles, electric utilities, industry, and home heating is primarily responsible for the increase in carbon dioxide. At the same time, worldwide deforestation has decreased nature's ability to remove atmospheric carbon dioxide through photosynthesis.[15]

Controversy has continued around the allegation that global warming was resulting from the build-up of greenhouse gases. The evidence now seems to demonstrate that global warming is indeed occurring. In 2001, the United States National Climate Data Center, a body of the National Oceanic and Atmospheric Administration, confirmed that global surface temperatures have in fact increased by 0.6°C since the late nineteenth century and 0.4°C during the past 25 years. Although global warming has not been uniform across the globe, as we have seen, 10 of the warmest 13 years since record-keeping began in the mid-nineteenth century have occurred since 1990. This increase of global temperature closely parallels the increase in atmospheric greenhouse gases. As was described in the previous section, since accurate data from scientific instruments was first available in the late 1800s, the 12 warmest years on record were, in descending order, 2005, 1998, 2002, 2003, 2004, 2001, 1997, 1995, 1990, 1999, 1991, and 2000.

The ecological, climatic, and human effects of global warming remain unknown. Many variables could affect the future consequences of global warming. The climatic role played by oceans, the polar ice caps, and clouds, as well as human decisions concerning pollution, deforestation, fossil-fuel use, and agriculture, all have the potential for either increasing or decreasing global warming. As a result, overall global warming produced by an increase in greenhouse gases may result in diverse climate and weather changes, including colder temperatures at some times and places. A worst-case scenario predicts a rise on ocean levels due to melting of snow and ice in the earth's polar regions, climatic shifts, worldwide droughts and famine, and massive extinction of plant and animal life. A best-case scenario would include a gradual adaptation to higher temperatures through shifts in population and agricultural centers.

Although some in the business community continue to raise doubts and foster skepticism about global warming, others have acknowledged its reality and are seeking ways to move forward to counter the trend. In a 1997 speech that attracted worldwide attention, John Browne, Chief Executive of BP, announced that:

> "The time to consider the policy dimensions of climate change is not when the link between greenhouse gases and climate change is conclusively proven . . . but when the possibility cannot be discounted and is taken seriously by the society of which we are part. We in BP have reached that point . . . there is now an effective consensus among the world's leading scientists and serious and well informed people outside the scientific community that there is a discernible human influence on the climate, and a link between the concentration of carbon dioxide and the increase in temperature. . . . Those are wide margins of error, and there remain large elements of uncertainty—about cause and effect . . . and even more importantly about the consequences. But it would be unwise and potentially dangerous to ignore the mounting concern."[16]

Energy

As the Bush Administration's proposals described in Chapter One make clear, our energy future is as controversial as it is uncertain. Along with food, energy production is tremendously influential both economically and ecologically. The production and use of energy also gives rise to a wide range of ethical issues.

Worldwide, there are four general energy options available, each of which can raise significant ethical and ecological challenges. We can continue to rely primarily on fossil fuels, presently estimated to account for more than 80 percent of worldwide energy use. Second, we could shift to greater reliance on nuclear energy. As we have seen, the Bush Administration favored a combination of these first two approaches. Third, we could develop alternative energy sources such as wind, solar, hydrogen, and geothermal power. Each of these three is essentially a supply approach. A fourth alternative would focus on conservation and energy efficiency and seek to decrease the overall demand for energy.

Continuing dependence on fossil fuels raises several major ethical issues. Ethical questions concerning our responsibilities to future generations are raised by the fact that fossil fuels are a nonrenewable energy source so that every barrel of oil or ton of coal burned today is forever lost to future generations. Furthermore, the by-products of fossil fuel combustion pose hazards to both present and future generations.

There are real concerns that global production of oil is nearing its peak, with the prospect only of less oil available in the coming years. There is strong evidence suggesting that availability of fossil-fuel energy resources is decreasing significantly. At the same time, global demand for those resources, especially from China, India, and other developing countries, is increasing significantly.

The recognition of this convergence of decreasing supply and increasing demand was at the center of a recent call from the Chairman and CEO of Chevron-Texaco for changes in U.S. energy policy. In a speech delivered in February 2005, David J. O'Reilly claimed that we are now in the midst of what he called a "new energy equation."

> The most visible element of this new equation is that relative to demand, oil is no longer in plentiful supply. The time when we could count on cheap oil and even cheaper natural gas is clearly ending. Why is this happening now? . . . *Demand from Asia is one fundamental reason* for this new age of more volatile and higher prices. The Chinese economy alone is a roaring engine whose thirst for oil grew by more than 15 percent last year and will double its need for imported oil between 2003 and 2010—just seven years. This new Asian demand is reshaping the marketplace. And we're seeing the center of gravity of global petroleum markets shift to Asia and, in particular, to China and India. . . . *But demand isn't the only factor at play. Simply put, the era of easy access to energy is over.* In part, this is because we are experiencing the convergence of geological difficulty with geopolitical instability. Although political turmoil and social unrest are less likely to affect long-term supplies, the psychological effect of those factors can clearly have an impact on world oil markets, which are already running at razor-thin margins of capacity. Many of the world's big production fields are maturing just as demand is increasing. The U.S. Geological Survey estimates the world will have consumed one-half of its existing conventional oil base by 2030. Increasingly, future supplies will have to be found in ultradeep water and other remote areas, development projects that will ultimately require new technology and trillions of dollars of investment in new infrastructure.[17] [emphasis added]

Nuclear energy also faces major ethical challenges. Nuclear power generates toxic wastes that remain hazardous for thousands of generations. Even assuming that the operation of nuclear power plants can be made safe, disposal of nuclear wastes can jeopardize the health and safety of countless future people. In 2005, there were 126 different sites within the United States that store high-level radioactive wastes and spend nuclear fuel. None of these sites was designed to hold this waste for the long-term. Initial plans were to ship these wastes to a single secure and safe federal site. In 1978, the U.S. Department of Energy began studying Yucca Mountain, located in a remote desert on federally protected land 100 miles northwest of Las Vegas, to determine if that site would be suitable as the long-term geologic repository for nuclear waste. Almost 30 years later, construction of this storage site, if it is going to occur at all, is still years away. Finally, the proliferation of nuclear technology that is necessary for generating nuclear energy also raises ethical concerns of international peace and security. Recent years have witnessed growing tensions between the United States and Iran and North Korea over the proliferation of nuclear technologies.

Energy sources such as solar, wind, hydrogen, and geothermal power are often proposed as renewable and non-polluting alternatives to fossil and nuclear fuels. But here, too, some ethical challenges must be faced. Over the short term, alternative energy sources will likely be more expensive relative to fossil and nuclear fuels. Such price differentials mean that safer and cleaner energy sources will more likely be available to wealthy countries and individuals, whereas the poor will continue to rely on more dangerous and polluting energy sources. As a result, questions need to be raised concerning equality and fairness in the distribution of alternative energy sources. Furthermore, development of these alternative technologies may require government subsidies and incentives, which can raise additional questions of freedom, fairness, and equality.

VALUES AND THE BIOSPHERE: PRAGMATISM AND DIVERSITY

As we reflect upon the ethical dimensions of these challenges, there is a temptation to seek a simple and clear principle of environmental ethics. Is there one ethical theory of principle that can guide our environmental decision-making? At first glance, the simple answer to this question seems to be "No." A wide-range of values is cited in response to the question: Why should anyone care about the biosphere? Humans value the environment on many grounds: moral, aesthetic, spiritual, symbolic, cultural, historical, and, of course, self-interest.

This variety of values has created some controversy within environmental ethics. Some environmental philosophers believe that rational consistency demands that these diverse values be unified into a single environmental ethic. Failing to do so seems to suggest that environmental values are irreconcilable and therefore relativistic. This, in turn, would seem to provide a rationale for ignoring claims of those who defend non-economic values of the biosphere.

Others are troubled by any attempt to ground environmental responsibility in self-interest. In Chapter Six, we examine what is often called "the business case for sustainability," an approach that many environmentalists consider imprudent. The fear is that ethical and environmental responsibilities based on business' self-interest will prove tenuous and untrustworthy.

But the diversity of environmental values is not the same thing as relativism. Just because there is a diversity of environmental values does not mean that these values are without rational support. Ethics need not be incompatible with self-interest. Values provide us with reasons for acting in one way rather than another. Environmental values provide reasons to both conserve for sustained use and preserve as undisturbed the biosphere in which all life exists. Both views may be reasonable and justified, although they seem incompatible.

The philosophic view adopted in this book can be thought of as a version of environmental pragmatism, an approach to environmental values that shifts the focus of ethics away from what is *true* to what is *practical*. Pragmatists recognize that practical rationality, reasoning about what we ought to *do*, is different from theoretical rationality, reasoning about what is *true*. Ethics is fundamentally practical, its standard is practical rationality rather than theoretical rationality. Pragmatism understands that practical reasoning seldom offers unambiguous guidance in deciding what to do, and acknowledges that there can be multiple, and sometimes conflicting, reasons for our decisions.

The environmental pragmatism that I adopt holds that there are many good reasons for protecting the biosphere from continued unconstrained exploitation. This pragmatism holds that solutions to the challenges of sustainability in the United States may be very different from reasonable solutions in Kenya or Bangladesh. There may be many paths to environmental sustainability, and a pragmatic resolution can satisfy diverse values. In this context, pragmatism allows for the possibility that different business, different industries, different social, political, and cultural circumstances, might develop different, but equally valid, sustainable practices.

Pragmatism holds that diverse values can be equally reasonable, and, therefore, pragmatism encourages the tendency toward tolerance, compromise, respect, listening, and simply getting along. Pragmatic rationality values intellectual and moral openness, intellectual and moral care, and attention to details. These values prevent the pragmatic approach from collapsing into value relativism. With this pragmatic approach, the worry is that environmental philosophy is so focused on abstract conceptual issues that it has become irrelevant to the pressing concerns of environmental policy. On this view, it is time for philosophers to be more concerned with real-world practical issues such as pollution, environmental destruction, and environmental justice. Philosophers should come down out of the clouds (to use Aristophenes' image of Socrates) and become more pragmatic.

So what are some of the diverse values supporting a more ethically sensitive approach to the biosphere? The most obvious and immediate is the value of self-interest. Human beings need clean air and water, safe food, a moderate climate, an ozone layer, and productive soil to survive. It is in our self-interest, therefore, not to pollute, degrade, or destroy the biosphere.

Even for those of us in the developed world whose wealth enables us to have a secure supply of such necessities, self-interest provides good reasons to value a healthy global biosphere. First, of course, environmental boundaries seldom match political boundaries. Diverting rivers or draining aquifers for irrigation in one country effects farmers in neighboring countries. Water and air pollution migrate downstream and downwind. The atmosphere, the oceans, the climate, air, water, soil—all the basic physical elements of the biosphere—are truly common goods. Threats to them anywhere are threats to everyone. A similar point can be made about self-interested reasons to alleviate poverty. A common maxim, cited previously, is that poverty anywhere is a threat to prosperity everywhere.

Some self-interested reasons for valuing the biosphere involve immediate, short-term concerns. Tens of thousands of people in New England are being harmed by the loss of the local fishing industry brought about by the collapse of north Atlantic fisheries. Farming communities, and the consumers who depend on them for plentiful and affordable food, are being harmed by the loss of topsoil and groundwater. Millions of people are exposed on a daily basis to toxic chemicals and pollutants. Other self-interested reasons are longer-term: climate change, depletion of the earth's ozone layer, a peaking of world oil supplies.

Global environmental concerns can be connected to self-interest of business, especially business in an increasingly global economy, in many ways. Most generally, the long-term supply of the labor, capital, and natural resources necessary for production, as well as stable markets for its goods and services, provide many reasons to be concerned about long-term sustainability.

Beyond reasons of our own self-interest, the interests of future generations—our children, grandchildren, and more distant descendents—provide other even longer-term reasons to value the biosphere. Most directly, the health and safety of our children and grandchildren are being jeopardized by decisions that we are making today. In one dramatic situation, we are quite literally poisoning our own children. In one study, researchers discovered an average of 91 industrial chemicals, with a total of 167 different chemicals total, in the breast milk of a group of nine women in six states.[18]

Longer term, we are also putting future generations at risk. It may well be the case that no one presently living will suffer from the nuclear wastes now being stored on-site at every nuclear power plant in the world or now being generated by the world's military programs. But someone, somewhere, within the next 10,000 years that such wastes will remain deadly, is likely to suffer. Moreover, the type of people our children and grandchildren will become—the experiences open to them, the challenges and opportunities they face, the things and experiences they will value—will depend on the type of world they inherit from us. If they do not know about wilderness areas, or black rhinos, or the cod or swordfish, they will not miss them at all. But they will have been denied the opportunity to know of such things, and that is a loss. Destroying the earth's biological and natural diversity is no less a crime against our descendents than would be the destruction of the world's greatest artistic and cultural artifacts.

Virtually every ethical tradition would support strong ethical responsibilities to protect the interests of the next generations by preserving a healthy and stable biosphere. Matters of justice and rights, overall utility and happiness, care and love for our children, all call us to act now in ways that will prevent harm to our near-term ancestors.

Of course, the self-interest of human beings is not the only reason to value the biosphere. The biosphere is useful to us, and in this way has significant instrumental value. But many argue that the biosphere itself, or particular members of it, have an intrinsic value that deserves respect. Many argue that animals deserve moral consideration and respect. The way factory farms raise and slaughter the millions of cattle, pigs, and chickens inflicts significant pain and suffering on these animals. Many people consider this unethically cruel and unjust. Even if a food or agricultural business does not share these values, prudence alone provides a good reason for taking this view seriously.

Beyond ethical considerations, a wide-range of other value perspectives would support the conclusion that we recognize the intrinsic value of natural objects. Sometimes these values can be expressed in the marketplace, and, therefore, sometimes market demands can direct economic and business attention to them. But typically they are not, and such values can therefore be lost in a world dominated by conventional economic wisdom. The aesthetic value of wilderness areas, open spaces, biodiversity, forests, prairies, lakes, and shorelines provides important reasons to protect such things. The spiritual and religious values that many people find in nature, in biodiversity, and in undisturbed landscapes provide other reasons. Many elements of the biosphere have historical, cultural, or symbolic value. The bald eagle in America, the Ganges River in India, Serengeti Plain in Africa all have significant cultural meaning for many people. Treating them merely as resources to be used for economic growth would destroy something of immense value.

Given these pluralistic and pragmatic conclusions, a legitimate question is "Where, exactly, do we go from here?" Assuming that there is no unambiguous and dominant theory of environmental ethics to guide us, does the pluralistic and pragmatic solution provide any guidance? Are we left simply to muddle our way into the future?

I believe that the concept of sustainability can provide a rationally defensible and practical guide for future business policy. Sustainability acknowledges the diversity of human values, and thus is willing to make compromises. Sustainable development treats the biosphere as a home of resources to be used. Thus, strict preservationists and animal rights defenders may see it as unprincipled. Providing for the poor and disenfranchised may well require more rather than less use of wilderness areas and animal agriculture. Yet a sustainable future recognizes those values that make life worth living. A life without beauty, open space, biological diversity, and wild nature is not worth sustaining.

Endnotes

1 The political and rhetorical reality is that many resources are dismissed as biased because they present unwelcome news. Public interest groups, NGOs, environmental advocacy groups, and even United Nations agencies may have little credibility with defenders of the status quo. Readers are encouraged to do their own research with a healthy dose of skepticism about all claims. Science, as the great arbitrator of empirical truth, is always a good place to start.

2 Donella Meadows, et al., *The Limits to Growth* (New York: Universe Books, 1972). See also Donealla Meadows, et al., *Beyond the Limits* (Post Mills, Vermont: Chelsea Green Publishing, 1992).

3 *Report of the World Food Summit: Five years later* (United Nations, Food and Agriculture Organization, 2002) http://www.fao.org/DOCREP/MEETING/005/Y7106E/Y7106E00.HTM

4 http://www.worldbank.org/poverty/

5 http://www.cdc.gov/nccdphp/dnpa/index.htm

6 A.L. Aspelin, *Pesticide Industry Sales and Usage: 1994 and 1995 market estimates* (Washington, D.C.: Office of Prevention, Pesticides and Toxic Substances, U.S. EPA, 1997), as quoted in Solomon, G, et al., *Pesticides and Human Health: A Resource for Health Care Professionals* (Santa Monica, CA: Physicians for Social Responsibility, 2000), p. 9.

7 From Solomon, *op. cit.*, page 9.

8 The known cancer and reproductive claims are from Office of Environmental Health and Hazard Assessment, *List of chemicals known to the state to cause cancer or reproductive toxicity* (Sacramento, CA: California Environmental Protection Agency, 1998). The residue claim is from Solomon, *op. cit.*, p. 9, which cites three separate scientific studies.

9 Pimental, David, et al. 1992. Environmental and Economic Cost of Pesticide Use, *BioScience*, Vol. 42, No.10, 750–60.

10 Postel, Sandra, and Amy Vickers, "Boosting Water Productivity," in *State of the World 2004* (New York: Worldwatch Institute, 2004), Chapter 3.

11 See, for example, the U.S. Geological Service, http://pubs.usgs.gov/gip/deserts/desertification/.

12 http://www.fao.org/desertification/default.asp?lang=en

13 World Meteorological Organization, Statement on the Status of the Global Climate in 2003: "Global Temperature in 2003 Third Warmest" (Geneva, December 16, 2003) available at the WMO website, http://www.wmo.ch/; and "Global Temperature Trends," Goddard Institute for Space Studies, National Aeronautical and Space Administration, http://www.giss.nasa.gov/research/observe/surftemp/; http://data.giss.nasa.gov/gistemp/2005/.

14 United Nation's Food and Agriculture Organization, *State of the World Fisheries and Aquaculture (SOFIA report)* 1995 and annually.

15 A very insightful analysis of this issue within the context of business ethics can be found in Denis Arnold and Keith Bustos, "Global Climate Change" *Business and Professional Ethics Journal* Vol. 24, nos. 1 & 2, Spring 2006.

16 Climate Change Speech, by John Browne, Group Chief Executive, British Petroleum (BP America), Stanford University, May 19, 1997.

17 "U.S. Energy Policy: A Declaration of Interdependence," remarks by David J. O'Reilly, Chairman and CEO, Chevron-Texaco Corporation. Keynote address to the 24th annual CERA Week Conference, Houston, Texas February 15, 2005 available on the Chevron-Texaco website: http://www.chevrontexaco.com/news/speeches/2005/2005-02-15_oreilly.asp

18 Further studies along this line can be found in "The Epidemiology of Toxic Stews" by O. Wasserman, *Acta Oncol.* 1991; 30 (6 Spec No):15–25. See, also, "Toxic Breast Milk?" by Florence Williams, New York Times Magazine, Jan. 5, 2005.

chapter three

Economic Growth, Free Markets, and Business Responsibility

INTRODUCTION

The most influential and widespread approach to the global challenges outlined in Chapters One and Two is the economic theory of free markets and economic growth. Conventional wisdom suggests that the market and the law are adequate public policy tools. From this perspective, the economic growth that follows from free markets is the best approach—economically, ecologically, and ethically the best—for addressing worldwide problems.

In Chapter One, we referred to this approach as the "conventional wisdom" or the "reigning economic paradigm." It is fair to describe this paradigm as the default position for such international financial institutions as the World Bank, the International Monetary Fund, and most global trade agreements and treaties. The assumption is that societies can grow their way out of such economic, ecological, and ethical challenges.

This standard economic theory has direct implications for the social responsibility of business. Business should seek to maximize profits within the law. Doing this will ensure that business contributes to economic growth and thereby responds to society's needs as expressed through consumer demand and legal regulation. From this perspective, business executives can fulfill their social responsibility by pursuing profits within the law and within certain minimal moral side-constraints.

Although this model continues to dominate the thinking of many people and many institutions, there are good reasons for concluding that it will prove inadequate on economic, ecological, and ethical grounds. In this chapter, we describe the conventional wisdom regarding the standard economic model and the theory of corporate social responsibility that follows from it in some detail. To fully understand where we stand at present it is helpful to understand the thinking that brought us here. Chapter Four offers an ethical evaluation of these perspectives and makes the case for the need to re-conceptualize our standard model for thinking about business and economics. We begin by turning to how the standard model addresses each of the three areas of sustainability: economics, environment, ethics.

ECONOMIC GROWTH AS THE ECONOMIC GOOD

In addressing the economic challenges of the contemporary world, the standard model takes overall economic growth, typically understood in terms of Gross Domestic Product (GDP), as the measure of a society's economic well-being. The more goods and services that are produced within a society, the better off it is. Thus, to reduce poverty, the economy must grow. To keep pace with rising population, the economy must grow. To provide adequate food, the economy must grow. To provide clothing, shelter, health care, and education, the economy must grow. When we increase the amount of overall economic activity, we raise the standard of living and improve the quality of life. More goods and services mean that people will be in a better position to acquire those things that they need. In turn, the standard model argues that the most efficient and dependable means to achieve the goal of economic growth is to rely on the workings of a free and competitive market.

The roots of this model of economics and business can be traced to the eighteenth century writing of Adam Smith. In his *The Wealth of Nations* (1776), Smith provided a vision of economic prosperity that rejected the mercantilism that was common throughout eighteenth century Europe. At the dawn of the first industrial revolution, Smith concluded that specialization, free trade, and competition would lead to a rise in a nation's overall wealth. If individuals are left alone to pursue their own self-interest within a free and competitive market, their own self-interest rather than governmental social planning would lead, as if directed by an invisible hand, to the greater good for society.

The central idea of this model can be understood with an example of a simple farmer's market. Imagine that each Saturday morning regional farmers bring their crops into a central marketplace where they offer them for sale. From an overall social perspective, the optimal situation occurs when all the participants, both buyers and sellers, get as much of what they want as possible. The optimal outcome has the farmers selling their crops for as much money as possible, and the buyers getting as much of the produce that they want for as low a cost as possible.

Each farmer sets her price with several factors in mind. At a minimum, she wants to recover the costs of production: the labor, the seeds, the bank loan, and so forth. Beyond that, she knows that she cannot set a price higher than other farmers who are selling the same crop without losing the sale. The farmers therefore are in competition; whoever can produce the crops most efficiently—that is, at the lowest cost—is able to set the lowest asking price and therefore will achieve the sale. Likewise, consumers are in competition, both with the farmers and with each other. Consumers bargain with farmers over the asking price, seeking the lowest possible price for the best possible produce. Consumers also are in competition with each other. The late-arriving consumer has fewer choices and therefore pays a higher price for lower quality goods. The consumer who is more efficient in his own field of work will have more money to spend than others and therefore will be in a better relative position to buy the produce that he wants.

In such a market, an individual is able to improve her own position only when she can find another individual willing to make an exchange. Similarly, that second individual will make such an exchange only when he himself is made better-off by it. Left alone, individuals will constantly seek to improve their own position by seeking exchanges with others who are also seeking to improve their own positions. A marketplace is simply the occasion for such exchanges. Exchanges occur only when both parties are made better-off. Free individuals simply would not agree to an exchange unless they perceived that they would be better off by doing so. The more exchanges that occur, the more the community approaches the point at which it has an optimal allocation of the available resources, the ideal point at which as many people get as much of what they want as possible.

Thus, free individuals seeking their own self-interest, left alone within a marketplace, will constantly work to improve their own position and thereby improve the overall well-being of society. This observation led Smith to conclude, in one of the most famous passages in economic history, that:

> "Every individual necessarily labors to render the annual revenue of the society as great as he can. He generally indeed neither intends to promote the public interest, nor knows how much he is promoting it. . . . He intends only his own gain, and he is in this, as in many other cases, led by an invisible hand to promote an end which was no part of his intention. . . . By pursuing his own interest he frequently promotes that of the society more effectually than when he really intends to promote it. I have never known much good done by those who affected to trade for the public good."[1]

Two additional factors work to improve the efficiency of the marketplace. First, specialization will increase overall productivity. If each farmer tries to grow every crop for which there is a demand, efficiency will be less than if farmers specialized in growing a limited variety of crops. A division of labor in which individuals specialize in productive activities will increase overall production. Smith's famous example of productivity within a pin factory makes this point.

> "Those ten persons, therefore, could make among them upwards of forty-eight thousand pins in a day. Each person, therefore, making a tenth part of forty-eight thousand pins, might be considered as making four thousand eight hundred pins in a day. But if they had all wrought separately and independently, and without any of them having been educated to this peculiar business, they certainly

could not each of them have made twenty, perhaps not one pin in a day; that is, certainly, not the two hundred and fortieth, perhaps not the four thousand eight hundredth part of what they are at present capable of performing, in consequence of a proper division and combination of their different operations."[2]

But specialization is not enough to ensure greater overall efficiency. If a farmer specializes in a crop that his land is ill-suited for growing, efficiency would be lost rather than gained. Efficiency is improved when farmers specialize in crops that they are best able to grow on their land. If a farm is located on rocky soil in a hilly region, specializing in root crops makes less sense than dairy farming. Given that farmers are in competition, it is in a farmer's own best interest to specialize in those crops that she can produce more efficiently than her competitors. This comparative advantage would allow the farmer to price her crops lower and thereby to gain the sale. Specialization directed by comparative advantage is the second factor that significantly improves efficiency. Production should be moved to those best able, compared to others with whom they compete, to produce at the lowest costs. Producers benefit by being better able to sell their goods at a profit. Consumers benefit by having access to products at lower prices.

Thus, this simple example illustrates the rationale for competition, free trade, and free markets even on a global scale. Competition among rational and self-interested individuals will inevitably work toward efficient production and an optimal distribution of benefits. On a global scale, free trade will allow countries to attract those industries for which they enjoy a comparative advantage. Production should move to those regions where goods and services can be most efficiently produced. Countries should specialize in those industries and products that they can produce most efficiently. In this way, the global economy constantly works toward an optimal level of production, improving the overall economic well-being of all.

This model is reflected in the global economic realities of the past decade. Specialization and comparative advantage explain why Nike shoes are manufactured in Viet Nam, why Wal-Mart is the largest single trading partner of China, and why call centers for many American businesses and the basic tax-preparation for many American accounting firms are located in Bangalore, India.

Thus, the standard model defends a goal of economic growth for addressing global poverty and the personal and social harms that accompany poverty. Sustainable growth, from this perspective, would involve a balance between two opposing constraints. Worldwide productivity must be increased enough to result in an actual net per capita increase when adjusted for population growth and for inflation. Yet, growth must not be so fast that inflation becomes a problem by offsetting the per capita growth. Thus, steady economic growth without significant inflation is the standard model's version of sustainable development. As we explain in the following chapters, critics believe that the very concept of *growth* that underlies this approach is unsustainable.

FREE MARKET ENVIRONMENTALISM

This standard model also offers a comprehensive approach to answering contemporary environmental challenges. According to defenders, market mechanisms offer the most reasonable strategies for addressing such environmental concerns as resource conservation, pollution, and preservation. This conventional wisdom interprets environmental problems as economic problems and therefore as solvable by economic means. The fundamental environmental challenge, from this perspective, is to produce a clean and livable environment by efficiently allocating the costs and benefits of scarce resources.

Consider the market strategy on conserving resources. Many of the challenges reviewed in Chapter Two describe a case in which we are using too many resources too quickly. The argument is made that the biosphere is limited and that we have reached, or have already overshot, the biophysical limits of growth. The problem, therefore, is that we are running out of water, oil, forests, fertile topsoil, fisheries, minerals, and the like.

But the standard economic model has a response to such concerns. The economic law of supply and demand goes a long way toward explaining why resources will be conserved before being exhausted. The apparent problem of nonrenewable resources is less a problem than it appears. As the supply of a resource becomes scarcer, the price of that commodity becomes more expensive, causing demand to decline. Scarce resources will simply become too expensive to be completely depleted. Economics also teaches us that resources are substitutable, and, as the supply of one declines, the inevitable price increase creates an incentive for entrepreneurs to find and produce an alternative. Given the substitutability of resources, given the incentives provided by price increases as supplies dwindle, and given human creativity, we could conclude, in the words of economist Julian Simon, that "resources are infinite."[3]

This scenario was put to a test in 1980 when Julian Simon challenged Paul Ehrlich to place a bet on future commodity prices. Simon argued that if predictions about diminishing resources were correct, future prices of those resources will go higher as the supply decreased. If the market's analysis was correct, prices should remain level or even decline as alternatives were developed. Simon challenged Ehrlich to choose any five metals worth $1000 at 1980 prices. If, at the end of 10 years, the price (adjusted for inflation) for the same amount of these resources increased, Simon would send Ehrlich a check for the difference. If the prices fell, Ehrlich would send a check for the difference to Simon. Ehrlich agreed to the bet, and chose copper, chrome, nickel, tin, and tungsten. In 1990, Ehrlich sent Simon a check for $576.07, meaning that, adjusted for inflation, the price of these five commodities dropped by almost half.

Consider the example of copper that Simon cited in his case against Ehrlich. In a theoretic sense, the amount of physical copper on earth is finite. But as a resource to be used, copper, in a practical sense, is infinite. In 1980, copper commonly was used to manufacture pots and pans, plumbing, and telephone wire. As copper resources were used, and the price increased, incentives were created to develop alternatives. Stainless steel pots and pans could replace the more expensive copper, and as microwave ovens developed, the use of metal for cooking decreased. PVC (polyvinyl chloride) pipes have replaced much of the copper piping used in plumbing. Fiber optics and wireless technology means that copper wires are no longer the primary conduit for telephones. Additionally, recycling has also contributed to the global supply of copper. Using price as the measure for world supply of copper, given that the inflation-adjusted price of copper has declined, we should conclude that the worldwide supply of copper has increased over the past few decades.

The market approach offers a similar strategy for protecting resources such as clean air and water for which no substitutes are readily available. Human creativity notwithstanding, air and water, unlike copper, are not easily replaceable. Nonetheless, market forces will guarantee that humans will get all the clean air and water that they need. The market will work to find an optimal level of pollution.[4]

Defenders of the market point out that pure water exists nowhere in nature and that the concept of pure air is misguided. Pure H_2O might be found in laboratories, but every river, stream, lake, aquifer, and ocean has always contained bacteria and microbial life, minerals, and a variety of suspended materials. The earth's atmosphere contains a mixture of gases and materials. Rather than seeking pure air or water, the only reasonable public policy goal is to ensure that air and water are safe enough to breathe and to drink. We could, of course, try to make the earth's atmosphere and all of its rivers, lakes, and aquifers more pure than necessary for our use. But this would require spending significant resources on something that, from a health and safety perspective, is unnecessary. Air and water that is too clean would be a waste of resources that could be more useful elsewhere. We could work to produce ultra-clean air and water, but we would have to forsake other social projects to attain it. The fact that the public does not demand such action suggests that devoting resources to attain a goal beyond what is needed for safe air and water would be a waste of scare resources. Too little pollution, in the sense that other sacrifices would be made to attain this goal, would be a bad thing. There are acceptable levels of pollution. Likewise, too much pollution would be a bad thing. Thus, the goal of pollution policy should be to find the optimal level of pollution, the level at which the risks associated with the pollution are judged acceptable.[5]

Consider as an illustration the most pressing water pollution issue in many agricultural regions. Nitrates and nitrites are any of a wide variety of nitrogen and oxygen molecules that combine with both organic and inorganic compounds. Nitrates are a known health risk that can cause serious illnesses, especially in children. The primary sources of much nitrate and nitrite pollution in groundwater are the manure and fertilizers that are produced and used on farms.

Clearly, having too many nitrates and nitrites in our drinking water is unacceptable. Drinking water should be clean enough to drink without harm. Public policy could strive to remove all traces of nitrates and nitrites from drinking water. For example, a variety of treatment and filtration systems can remove these pollutants. We could also address the pollution at its source, by prohibiting the use of fertilizers and significantly regulating the use and storage of manure. Any of these options would require major expenditures and would certainly result in a rise in dairy and farm products.

The market approach argues that the pricing mechanism of markets is the most efficient method for determining the proper standard for acceptable risk. Ultimately, individuals should decide for themselves how much they are willing to pay for dairy and farm products to reduce the level of nitrates and nitrites in their drinking water. No other method for assessing the acceptable level of risk is as efficient.

The market paradigm also has strategies available for dealing with the preservation of highly valued resources, such as forests, wilderness areas, and endangered species. Within society, there are competing and conflicting demands for scarce resources. For example, forests are in demand to provide timber for logging, recreational areas for use for ATVs (all-terrain vehicles), snowmobiles, hiking and skiing, areas for fishing and hunting, habitat for wildlife, and scenic and wild areas for aesthetic and spiritual reasons. Public policy must find a way to balance these conflicting demands, and the market does just that. Market mechanisms can, in the words of one advocate, provide Americans with "all the wilderness, timber, wildlife, fish, and other forest resources they want." [6] The goal is to find the optimal balance of the competing demands for various resources. Once again, this goal can be achieved through the prices established by supply and demand.

The most ideological defenders of the market would argue for privatization of all resources as the most efficient means for attaining the optimal balance among competing uses. Private owners, seeking their own best interests, would be motivated to ensure that such resources would go to those who most value them, in the sense of those willing to pay most for the resources. Less ideological advocates would allow that government regulation and control of some public goods would also contribute to sound environmental policy.

Consider a resource such as Yellowstone Park. Some people want it preserved as a wilderness area. Others would like to develop hotels and other commercial enterprises in the park. Some desire to use snowmobiles to access the backcountry during winter months; others oppose any motorized vehicles that could disturb elk, bison, and other wildlife. Some supported the reintroduction of wolves into the park; others opposed it.

A strict market solution to these conflicting demands would be to allocate this scarce resource on the basis of price. Presumably, this would entail establishing a market for the various uses. Perhaps an auction could be established at which the various constituencies would bid against themselves to acquire the right to use the park as they desire. Supply and demand of the various uses would eventually establish the point at which all uses have as much of the resource as they want, or at least as they are willing to pay for. As areas available for snowmobiling increase, and areas available for skiing decrease, the price for snowmobiling permits would decline, and the price of skiing permits would increase to the point at which skiers would be outbidding snowmobilers for access to the park. Ultimately, supply and demand competition would work out an optimal distribution in which the overall society gets all that it wants. In this manner, the scarce resource is allocated in the most optimal way to those who most value it.

The concept of privatization plays a central role in the market approach to many other environmental concerns, particularly those involving renewable resources. Economics has long recognized the problem of the commons. Unowned goods, goods held "in common," are ripe for exploitation. If no one owns a resource, everyone who wants to use it has an incentive to take as much of it as possible, before others have a chance to do so. For renewable resources, this strategy could have tragic consequences. The commons provides an incentive to deplete resources faster than they can be renewed. Also, if no one owns an area, there is also little incentive for people to refrain from using it as a dumping ground for waste. Lacking a property right interest in some area, no one has the incentive or ability to prevent others from degrading that area.

The American bison that roamed the plains in the nineteenth century is a classic example of this phenomenon. No one owned the bison, and therefore anyone could take as many as they wanted. This also meant, of course, that no one had any incentive to preserve the bison for later use or to prevent others from exploitation. Bison "preserved" by one hunter would be taken by another. Thus, everyone had an incentive to take as many as they could before others do so. The result, not surprisingly, was the near extinction of the bison. It was not until private individuals took possession of the remaining bison as private property that the population could be stabilized and extinction prevented. The population of this resource became sustainable only when it became privately owned.

Similar claims would be made for all animal species that are threatened with extinction, from whales and ocean fish species, to mountain gorillas and California condors. In every case, endangered species are unowned wild animals. The most plentiful animals—cows, chickens, dogs, cats—are privately owned. Private property rights create an incentive to protect one's property from overuse and exploitation. Owners have the ability to deny others access to the resource, thereby preventing overuse and exploitation. Owners have the incentive to treat environmental resources as capital from which to collect interest in the form of long-term sustainable harvest, rather than as income to be spent before it disappears.

For example, market defenders propose that ocean fisheries be auctioned off in the form of licenses or permits that allow the owner exclusive rights to harvest a particular species or to fish in a particular region. Such licenses would function in much the same way that the 200-mile limit surrounding coastal shorelines functions for countries. The right holder has legal authority to prevent others from operating within the defined limits. Once the fear of exploitation by others is removed, the license holder has every incentive to harvest fish at sustainable rates. This incentive means that fisheries would be treated as capital, from which a steady rate of return can be taken, rather than as income to be spent or a common resource to be exploited.

Thus, the market paradigm claims that economic growth and market forces can adequately address the economic and environmental challenges facing the world in the twentieth century. This paradigm also claims a strong ethical basis as well.

Free Market Ethics

Defenders of the market cite two major ethical traditions in support of their approach to economic and environmental challenges. This reigning paradigm appeals to the utilitarian principle of maximizing the overall good and the individual rights to liberty and private property for its ethical justification.

Utilitarianism judges the ethical legitimacy of action or policy in terms of the consequences that follow from it. If some act or policy produces greater overall good than the alternatives, it is ethically justified. In turn, the goodness of the consequences is understood in terms of individual happiness. Thus, an act that tends to increase the overall amount of individual happiness is ethically justified; one that tends to decrease overall happiness is ethically wrong.

The utilitarian ethical tradition, like neoclassical economics itself, traces its roots to such eighteenth and nineteenth century thinkers as Adam Smith, Jeremy Bentham, and John Stuart Mill. This tradition argued that impartiality and equality were fundamental requirements of ethics. No individual person or individual class was more worthy than another. Each person was to count for one and only one. Society ought not to be arranged in any way that would benefit one group at the expense of others. Therefore, the only plausible criteria by which social policy could be judged are *overall* consequences. Social policy is ethically justified if it produces the greatest good for the greatest number; it is unjustified otherwise.

It was part of Adam Smith's greatest insight that he understood the role that free and competitive markets can play in attaining this goal. Individuals may well be egoists in that they tend to seek their own personal self-interest. But society need not expect individuals to be altruists in order to attain ethical results. Social institutions can be structured in a way that translates individual egoism to the greater overall good. Competitive markets are just that social structure that can transform, as if "led by an invisible hand," individual self-interest into the public good.

The major alternative approach to ethics cites individual rights rather than overall consequences as the fundamental ethical value. Utilitarianism is a collectivist ethics in that it judges right and wrong in terms of the consequences to the overall group. An alternative approach emphasizes the inherent dignity of each individual, a dignity best protected by individual rights. Respect for individual rights, rather than promoting the overall good, is the more important value according to this tradition.

Although utilitarianism and individual rights are sometimes cast as rival ethical theories, they are better understood as complementary approaches. Individual rights are best understood as establishing constraints on the more general pursuit of overall happiness. As an example, consider how constitutional rights can function within democracies. In general, a majority-rule and democratic decision procedure serves the overall good. Legislatures tend to adopt policies that promote majoritarian policies that serve the greater good for the greatest number. Constitutional rights act as checks upon and establish boundaries for majority-favored policies. We should not violate individual rights, even if doing so would produce greater overall happiness. We should promote the greatest overall good, as long as no rights are violated in the process.

Defenders of the economics of free markets appeal to two important rights in the defense of their views. Both the right of individual liberty and the right to private property provide strong support for market economics. An individual's right to liberty is understood as the right to be free from interference, what is usually identified as *negative liberty*. This libertarian tradition argues that the best way to respect the dignity of every individual is to allow individuals to make their own decisions. Logically, we must extend this same right to everyone, and therefore the right to individual liberty is more precisely understood as the right to make one's own decisions as long as those decisions do not interfere with the equal rights of others to make their own. More simply, liberty is understood as the right to be free from the interference of others.

Libertarians next argue that the only social and economic arrangement that is consistent with and protects individual liberty is a minimal government and free market economy. Governments should protect the rights of their citizens, prevent force and coercion, prohibit fraud, and otherwise stay out of the lives of their citizens. Markets free from government control and regulation allow individuals to decide for themselves how they choose to live their lives. From this ethical perspective, such an arrangement best respects the dignity of each individual.

Finally, the standard model appeals to a right to privately own and control property as an ethical justification. John Locke, for example, argued that along with life and liberty, property is among the basic natural rights. Given this, free market capitalist economies once again appear to be the only economic systems that fully respect that right.

CORPORATE SOCIAL RESPONSIBILITY AND THE STANDARD MODEL

This standard model of market economics has direct implications for the social responsibilities of business. What is often referred to as the classic model of corporate social responsibility (CSR) argues that business managers have a primary responsibility to maximize profits within the law. Doing this will ensure that business institutions will fulfill their economic function of allocating resources to those who most value them and their ethical responsibility to respect the rights of business owners for whom they work.

Economist Milton Friedman has offered the best-known defense of this position. In his book *Capitalism and Freedom*, Friedman summarizes his view as follows:

> The view has been gaining widespread acceptance that corporate officials . . . have a social responsibility that goes beyond serving the interests of their stockholders . . . This view shows a fundamental misconception of the character and nature of a free economy. In such an economy, there is one and only one social responsibility of business—to use its resources and engage in activities designed to increase its profits so long as it stays within the rules of the game, which is to say, engages in open and free competition, without deception or fraud . . . . Few trends could so thoroughly undermine the very foundations of our free society as the acceptance by corporate officials of a social responsibility other than to make as much money for their stockholders as possible.[7]

By trying to "make as much money as possible," corporate managers will ensure that the resources being used in their businesses will go to those uses most highly valued by a society. The constraints on this pursuit, that the competition must be "open and free" and "without deception and fraud" are, as Freidman suggests, part of "the rules of the game." That is, markets that are not "open and free" or that are characterized by "deception and fraud" will fail to achieve the economic ends for which they were designed.

These limitations on the pursuit of profits are internal to the economic system itself. Profits earned fraudulently or through monopolistic practices, for example, are illegitimate.

In a later statement of his views, Freidman offers a formulation that differs in a slight, but very significant, way.

> "In a free-enterprise, private property system a corporate executive is an employee of the owners of the business. He has direct responsibility to his employers. That responsibility is to conduct the business in accordance with their desires, which generally will be to make as much money as possible while confirming to the basic rules of society, both those embodied in law and those embodied in ethical custom . . . The key point is that, in his capacity as a corporate executive, the manager is the agent of the individuals who own the corporation . . . and his primary responsibility is to them."[8]

This formulation is significantly different because the range of constraints on the pursuit of profits has been expanded to include the obligations to obey the law and "ethical customs." This change has the potential to completely undermine Friedman's initial thesis. If the law or ethical custom is interpreted broadly enough, the responsibility to make as much money as possible is no longer the "one and only one" nor the "primary" social responsibility of business.

In many ways, this is the central issue in debates concerning CSR. One can think of the competing models of CSR along a continuum of expanding the legal and ethical constraints upon the goal of maximizing profits. At one extreme, we find the very narrow view of CSR associated with neoclassical economics and Friedman's initial formulation. Business's social responsibility is to maximize profit by meeting consumer demand, and the only constraint is the duty to obey the rules of the economic game, compete fairly, and avoid deception and fraud. At its most libertarian extreme, this view would argue that the only appropriate legal constraints are those that protect property and prohibit fraud and coercion.

Theories of CSR become more moderate, although still remaining within the general framework of market economics, by expanding the range of constraints upon the pursuit of profit. Friedman's later version acknowledges additional duties to obey the law and ethical custom. More recently, Norman Bowie explicates such "ethical customs" on Kantian grounds to include the moral duty to cause no harm, even if such acts are not prohibited by law.[9] In 1991, Bowie claimed that "something of a consensus has emerged in the past ten years regarding the social responsibility of business." Bowie labels this consensus the "neoclassical" model of corporate social responsibility. On this model, the pursuit of profit is constrained by an obligation to obey a "moral minimum." Business managers must first meet certain moral obligations that, once met, open the door to the pursuit of profit.[10]

To explain this notion of a "moral minimum," Bowie appeals to a framework for distinguishing duties that is fairly standard in traditional ethical theories. In simple terms, this framework distinguishes between ethical imperatives to cause no harm, to prevent harm, and to do good. People have a strong ethical duty to cause no harm, and only a *prima facie* duty to prevent harm and an even less strict duty to do good. Doing good is something that people should be encouraged to do and praised for doing. But it is not something that people are ethically obligated to do, because such an obligation would impose unreasonable burdens and limitations on individual freedom. The obligation to cause no harm, on Bowie's view, overrides other ethical considerations. The pursuit of profit legitimately can be constrained by this ethical duty. On the other hand, Bowie accepts the classic model's view that managers are the agents of stockholder-owners and thus they have a duty (derived from the contract between them) to further the interests of stockholders. Thus, although it is ethically good for managers to prevent harm or to do some good, their duty to stockholders overrides these concerns. As long as managers comply with the moral minimum and cause no harm, they have a responsibility to maximize profits. In this way, the "neoclassical model" can be interpreted as a revised version of the classic model of corporate social responsibility.

We can thus characterize these standard theories as variations on the theme of balancing utilitarian and rights-based ethics. The pursuit of profit is the mechanism by which business is thought to serve the utilitarian goal of satisfying consumer demand and thereby maximizing the overall social good. This utilitarian goal is constrained by the duties that one has to persons affected by these activities. Our duties to other people (and their rights) create side-constraints or boundaries on business activity; as long as business does not overstep those boundaries, it is free to pursue profit. Depending on the theory of rights and duties that one adopts, those constraints range from the minimal duty of obeying the law to more extensive accounts of duties associated with various stakeholder theories of CSR.

CORPORATE ENVIRONMENTAL RESPONSIBILITY

It is fair to say that virtually all mainstream theories of corporate social responsibility (CSR) deny that business has any special environmental responsibilities. From the classic model of CSR associated with Milton Friedman and other defenders of the free market to the more recent stakeholder theory, environmental concerns function, at best, as side-constraints on business managers. Business may have some negative duties associated with the environment, duties not to pollute and not to cause harm, but business has no positive duty to conduct itself in ways that contribute to long-term ecological and environmental well-being. What one will not find among these common views is an account of CSR that holds that business has positive duties either to *prevent* ecological harm or *to do* environmental good.

Continuing the side-constraint and boundary metaphor, ethical goals do not determine either the direction or the substance of business activity. In essence, these views adopt an ethically passive model of business management in which managers can fulfill their responsibilities by actively doing little or nothing at all. Business passively *responds to* the demands of the market. Business is passive in *not violating the law*. Business is passive when it *causes no harm*. According to these views, the social responsibility of business requires business *to do* virtually nothing at all. Society has two opportunities to direct business toward social and environmental goals. Society can demand such things as consumers in the marketplace, and society can require such things by passing legislation as citizens. Aside from those two demands, business has no special social or environmental responsibilities.

Once again, Norman Bowie provides a clear statement of business' environmental responsibilities under the standard model.

> "As long as business obeys the environmental laws and honors other standard moral obligations, most harm done to the environment by business has been accepted by society. Through their decisions in the marketplace, we can see that most consumers are unwilling to pay extra for products that are more environmentally friendly than less friendly competitive products. Nor is there much evidence that consumers are willing to conserve resources, recycle, or tax themselves for environmental causes."[11]

Society sets the environmental agenda in two ways: consumer demand and governmental regulation. Business has no environmental responsibilities other than to respond to these dual mechanisms for conveying society's preferences.

Going beyond this moral minimum is something that would be morally praiseworthy, but it is not something that society can require or expect of business. Bowie distinguishes between *causing* harm, *preventing* harm, and doing good. Morality can require that business cause no harm, but it can require business to prevent harm only in exceptional circumstances. Bowie cites four such circumstances: capability, need, proximity, and last resort.[12] Like the Good Samaritan, we praise people who prevent harms that they did not cause, but seldom require it.

Consider, therefore, how this perspective would address issues of sustainability. Because no individual firm is causing such harms to the biosphere as global warming, species extinction, or resource depletion, acting to counter such harms is beyond the moral minimum. If the collective result of individual firms acting as they do threatens the biosphere, government should act to prevent such harms through legislation. If this is not required by law, business has no obligation to move in the direction of sustainability.

Several responses to this perspective will be developed in the following chapter. I suggest that this is too narrow an understanding of ethical responsibilities. I also argue that this view misrepresents the latitude business and managerial discretion, essentially creating a false dichotomy between sustainability and profit. Finally, I suggest that there are many good business reasons, ethical and financial, for business to move toward sustainability. Such reasons undermine the alleged conflict between ethics and self-interest that is assumed by this conventional perspective.

Endnotes

1 [An Inquiry into the Nature and Causes of the Wealth of Nations, vol. I, bk. IV, ch. 2.]

2 [*An Inquiry into the Nature and Causes of the Wealth of Nations* par. I.I.3]

3 Julian Simon, The Ultimate Resource (Princeton, NJ: Princeton University Press 1981).

4 This phrase is from William Baxter, *People or Penguins: The Case for Optimal Pollution* (New York, Columbia University Press, 1974).

5 Ibid., p. 8.

6 Randal O'Toole, *Reforming the Forest Service* (Washington, D.C.: Island Press, 1988), p. xii.

7 Milton Friedman, *Capitalism and Freedom* (Chicago: University of Chicago Press, 1962), p. 133.

8 Milton Friedman "The Social Responsibility of Business is to Increase Its Profits," The *New York Times Magazine* (September 13, 1970), p. 9.

9 See Norman Bowie, "Morality, Money, and Motor Cars," reprinted in DesJardins and McCall, eds., *Contemporary Issues in Business Ethics* 5th edition (Belmont, CA.: Wadsworth Publishing, 2005), pp. 404–409.

10 Norman Bowie, *"New Directions in Corporate Social Responsibility,"* in *Business Horizons* (July–August 1991): 56. Bowie's views are developed further in his *Business Ethics: A Kantian Perspective* (Oxford, Blackwell, 1999).

11 Bowie, "Morality, Money, and Motor Cars," p. 406.

12 Ibid., p. 405.

chapter four

The Failure of Market-Based Policies

INTRODUCTION

Standard models of corporate social responsibility presuppose the legitimacy of a growth-based, market economy. These views treat market-based solutions as the default position. As long as minimal moral requirements are satisfied, whatever social policy from the workings of competitive markets is ethically acceptable. Business need only obey the law, respect moral minimums, and respond to the demands expressed within the market. Left alone, efficient markets and economic growth best serve social goals. Ethical and legal responsibilities function as side-constraints upon the economic goals that follow from the role of business institutions within the neoclassical economic model.

The question of the environmental responsibilities of business comes down to the question of whether or not such models of corporate social responsibility can adequately address the economic, environmental, and ethical requirements for a sustainable society. Can the economic, environmental, and ethical challenges outlined in Chapter Two be left to the workings of competitive markets or brought within the moral minimum? Will an ethically adequate environmental policy be achieved when such responsibilities function as side-constraints on the goal of economic growth? I believe that an adequate environmental ethic for business is possible only if environmental responsibility functions not as a side-constraint upon normal business activities, but as shaping the very nature of how business is conducted. In short, any view that leaves the fulfillment of environmental responsibilities to the undirected workings of competitive markets will prove inadequate on a variety of ethical and environmental grounds.

CRITIQUE OF GROWTH-BASED MARKET MODEL:
INTERNAL CHALLENGES

Extensive criticism has been raised against the legitimacy of markets as tools for setting environmental (or any public) policy. A complete review of such criticism would be beyond the scope of this chapter. However, two general challenges to the ethical and environmental legitimacy of such a reliance on markets establish a fairly conclusive case.

Even the strongest defenders of markets acknowledge the existence of a variety of market failures. Particularly relevant for our concern is the existence of externalities, the textbook example of which is environmental pollution. Because the "costs" of such things as air pollution, groundwater contamination and depletion, soil erosion, and nuclear waste disposal are typically borne by parties "external" to the economic exchange (e.g., people downwind, neighbors, future generations), free market exchanges cannot guarantee optimal results.

A second type of market failure occurs when no markets exist to create a price for important social goods. Endangered species, scenic vistas, rare plants and animals, and biodiversity are just some environmental goods that typically are not traded on open markets (when they are, it often is in ways that seriously threaten their viability as when rhinoceros horns, tiger claws, elephant tusks, and mahogany trees are sold on the black market). Public goods such as clean air and ocean fisheries also have no established market price. The diverse intrinsic values described in Chapter Two cannot be measured by nor reduced to their exchange value. With no established exchange value, markets fail to guarantee that such goods are preserved and protected.

A third way in which market failures can lead to serious environmental harm involves a distinction between individual decisions and group consequences. Important ethical and policy questions can be missed if we leave policy decisions solely to the outcome of individual decisions. This problem arises for many issues, particularly for health risks involved in environmental concerns such as exposure to workplace chemicals, consuming food treated with pesticides, and drinking water that contains nitrates and chemical residues. As a particular example, consider the decision involved in choosing to drive a low-mileage sports utility vehicle.

Driving such vehicles significantly increases the amount of airborne pollutants discharged per mile driven. A 13 mpg SUV will discharge 134 tons of CO_2 over its 124,000-mile lifetime. A 36-mpg compact car will discharge 48 tons over the same distance. If I act as the rationally, self-interested individual presupposed by neoclassical economics, I would calculate the benefits of driving an SUV and weigh them against the increased costs and health risks that I face from pollution. Because the increased risks to me (or to any individual facing such a choice) of *my* driving an SUV rather than a compact are infinitesimally small, my self-interested choice to drive an SUV is reasonable according to market conceptions of individual rationality.

Consider these same facts not from an individual point of view but from the point of view of the population of, for example, Los Angeles. Because, as our individual calculation indicated, it can be rational for any individual to choose an SUV, the individualistic approach implicit in market solutions would accept the Los Angeles pollution rate as a rational policy.

The overall social result of such individual calculations might be significant increases in pollution and such pollution-related diseases as asthma and allergies. There are a number of alternative policies (e.g., restricting SUV sales, increasing taxes on gasoline, treating SUVs as cars instead of light trucks in calculating corporate automobile fuel efficiency (CAFE) standards, creating tax incentive for alternative fuel transportation), that could address pollution and pollution-related disease. However, these alternatives would only be considered if we examine this question from a social rather than individualistic perspective. Because these are important ethical questions, and because they remain unasked from within market transactions, we must conclude that markets are incomplete (at best) in their approach to the overall social good. In other words, what is good and rational for a collection of individuals is not necessarily what is good and rational for a society.

This point helps illuminate problems with the distinction between causing and preventing harm that was described in the previous chapter. Remember that this distinction supported the claim that business has no direct ethical obligation to prevent ecological harms that it did not cause. From the point of view of a consumer or firm, individual actions seldom if ever would cause the type of ecological harm that threatens the biosphere. But collectively, such actions cause real harms, and this provides reasons for each individual to refrain from acting in such ways.

These three types of market failure raise serious concerns for the ability of economic markets to achieve a sound environmental policy. As a consequence, any account of business' environmental responsibility that thinks that this responsibility will be satisfied simply by leaving business free to respond to market demands will be incomplete at best.

Of course, defenders of market solutions have ready responses to these challenges. Even free market defenders could support regulation that would require business to internalize externalities. Presumably they would support legislation to create shadow prices for unpriced social goods or for exempting such goods from the market, as when national parks and wilderness areas are set aside as public lands. A more adequate system of legal property rights is also often proposed as a response to threats to commonly unowned goods such as ocean fisheries and rare animals. The law is also the appropriate mechanism for addressing social goods that are unattainable through individual choice. In short, the law is the obvious remedy for environmental harms resulting from market failures. And, once again, as long as business obeys the law, it is meeting its environmental responsibility when it responds to consumer demand in the marketplace.

But there are good reasons for thinking that such *ad hoc* attempts to repair market failures are environmentally and ethically inadequate. First is what I call the first-generation problem. Markets, and government regulation that develops to correct market failures, can work to prevent harm only through information supplied by the existence of markets failures. Only when fish populations in the North Atlantic collapsed did we learn that free and open competition among the world's fishing industry for unowned public goods failed to prevent the decimation of cod, swordfish, Atlantic salmon, and lobster populations. That is, we learn about market failures and thereby prevent harms in the future only by sacrificing the "first-generation" as a means for gaining this information. When public policy involves irreplaceable public goods such as endangered species, rare wilderness areas, and public health and safety, such a passive and reactionary strategy is ill-advised.

Consider how this conventional wisdom would address the problem of toxic residues discovered in breast milk. As is the case in the U.S. system, business would be free to sell products treated with untested chemical compounds as long as these products are intended for neither food nor drug use. Over time, consumers would learn that these chemicals leave residues behind, in fatty tissue and in breast milk, for example. Conventional economic wisdom would then give consumers two opportunities to restrict the sale of such products: they could stop buying them and the reduced demand would eliminate the product, or they could lobby government to regulate them. But until such time as consumer demand or government regulation directs, business has no reason to restrict the production or use of these chemicals.

Unfortunately, the only process for obtaining the information that toxic chemical build-up in human tissues might pose a threat is by treating the first generation of consumers as guinea pigs. The price that society pays to get information about dangerous products is borne by those who are harmed by the product.

There is a modified version of this view in which government regulation establishes health and safety standards for all new products. Thus, once again, business would escape responsibility for the safety of its products. Many government regulations in the United States today, especially within such agencies that regulate consumer products and workplace safety, follow this model. But this approach alone, without a more active role for business, is inadequate for several reasons. First, social scientists have long recognized the problem of regulatory capture, a process in which regulators become "captured" by the industry they are designed to regulate. For a variety of reasons, ranging from corruption to the psychology involved in working with people on a daily basis, to the fact that government regulators usually rely on industry for the data and information used in regulation, regulators often fail to fulfill their mission to protect citizens. Second, if society relies on government alone to ensure the safety of products, the likely result would be many regulations and inefficient economies. Business is in a much better position than government both to understand and to take steps to avoid environmental damages caused by their products.

If we allow government regulation to establish environmental standards for business, we are still faced with the ability of business to influence both government regulation and consumer demand. The neoclassical model limits the environmental responsibility of business to obey the law and respond to consumer demand. On this model, it is government's responsibility to prevent and compensate for market failures. Once market failures are adequately addressed, business need only obey the law and respond to the market. But this assumes that business cannot or does not inappropriately influence the law. "Inappropriate" influence, on this model, is influence aimed not at optimizing the overall good (the goal, after all, of markets) but at protecting the interests of business. An obvious example is the automobile industry's successful lobbying effort to have SUVs treated as trucks rather than as passenger vehicles so that manufacturers can meet CAFE standards established by law.

To his credit, Norman Bowie recognizes the potential problem here and acknowledges that if business can be said to have any special environmental responsibility, it is to refrain from influencing the environmental standards of government. But just as we must recognize the ability of business to influence government policy, we must recognize the ability to influence consumers. To conclude that business fulfills its environmental responsibility when it responds to the environmental demands of consumers is to underestimate the role that business can play in shaping public opinion. Advertising is a $200 billion a year industry in the United States alone. It is surely disingenuous to claim that business passively responds to consumer desires and that consumers are unaffected by the messages that business conveys. Assuming that business is not going to stop advertising its products or lobbying government, the market-based approach to environmental responsibility that is implicit within both the classic and neoclassical model of corporate social responsibility is inadequate.

Furthermore, there are good reasons to minimize the range of ethical responsibilities enforced by law. The law functions best when it provides general targets for, and side-constraints upon, managerial discretion. The law is a crude tool to use to micromanage managerial decisions. It is preferable, on both economic and moral grounds, to expect business to meet its ethical responsibilities without having these mandated by law.

To understand the inadequacy of the law to prevent harms, consider the corporate scandals of recent years. It is worth remembering that many of the people involved in the wave of recent corporate scandals were lawyers. In the Enron case, for example, corporate attorneys and accountants were encouraged to "push the envelope" of what was legal. Especially in civil law, wherein much of the law is established by precedent, there is always room for ambiguity in applying the law. After all, every new case is different in some way from the previous. Additionally, in civil law there is a real sense in which one has not done anything illegal unless and until a court decides that one has, and this means that if no one files a lawsuit to challenge some action, it was legal.

To say that all a business needs to do is obey the law suggests that laws are clear-cut, unambiguous rules that can be easily applied. This rule model of law is very common, but not very accurate. If the law was clear and unambiguous, there would not be much of a role for lawyers and courts. If a corporate manager is told, as the standard model suggests, that she has a social responsibility to maximize profits within the law, as a responsible manager, she would consult her corporate attorneys and accountants to ask what the law allows. A competent attorney or accountant will advise on how far one can reasonably go before doing something that is obviously illegal. In this situation, it would seem that a manager has a responsibility to "push the envelope" of legality in pursuit of profits. Whatever is not obviously illegal is socially responsible.

Most of the cases of dramatic corporate scandal in recent years involved attorneys and accountants who advised their clients that what they were doing could be defended in court. The off-book partnerships that were at the heart of the collapse of Enron and Arthur Andersen were designed with the advice of attorneys who thought that, if challenged, they had at least a reasonable chance of winning in court. At this point, the decision to "push the envelope" becomes more a matter of risk-assessment and cost-benefit analysis than a matter of ethics. On this model, there is a strong incentive to assess the likelihood of being challenged in court, the likelihood of losing the case, the likelihood of settling for financial damages, and the comparison of those costs against the financial benefits of taking the action. This, I suggest, is not an adequate response to environmental and ethical challenges that can result in irreversible harms.

Finally, the assumption that the law can provide adequate solution to market failures and practical public policy guidance is rather peculiar in an age of global economic integration. Which law ought business firms obey in the pursuit of profits? The conventional model associated with Milton Friedman advises business to pursue profits within the law. This idea can sound attractive when situated in the context of stable democratic political structures. It is much less attractive ethically when situated in a repressive and corrupt political system. Friedman's advice to ignore one's own personal morality and simply pursue profits within the law would allow, indeed it would require, firms doing business in corrupt countries to employ child labor, dump toxic wastes, exploit national resources, displace communities, and destroy species and ecosystems.

Beyond the case of corrupt regimes, the fact is that there are very few binding international agreements or laws. In an increasingly integrated global economy, the advice to pursue profits within the law provides very little advice at all. To the degree that international agreements exist, they are agreements between nation-states and do not bind multinational corporations in the way envisioned by the theory of corporate social responsibility associated with free-market economics.

CRITIQUE OF GROWTH-BASED MARKET MODEL: EXTERNAL CHALLENGES

A more comprehensive challenge to the ability of markets to set reasonable environmental policy has been raised by economists working on sustainable development and ecological economics. Herman Daly, a leading figure in this field, makes a convincing case for an understanding of economic *development* that transcends the present standard of economic *growth*. There are, Daly argues, biological, physical, and ethical limits to growth, many of which the present world economy is already approaching, if not overshooting. Unless we make significant changes in our understanding of economic activity, unless quite literally we change the way we do business, we will fail to meet some very basic ethical and environmental obligations. According to Daly, we need a major paradigm shift in how we understand economic activity.

We can begin with the standard understanding of economic activity and economic growth found in almost every economics textbook.[1] What is sometimes called the "circular flow model" explains the nature of economic transactions in terms of a flow of resources from businesses to households and back again (see Figure A). Households invest their labor, skills, property, and capital in business. Business uses these inputs to produce goods and services in response to the market demands of households. These goods and services are shipped to households in exchange for payments back to business. These payments are in turn sent back to households in the form of wages, salaries, rents, profits, and interests. These payments are received by households in exchange for the labor, land, capital, and entrepreneurial skills that were originally sent to business to produce goods and services.

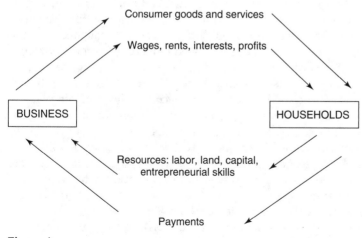

Figure A

Two items are worth noting at this point. First, natural resources are undifferentiated from the other factors of production. On this model, the origin of resources is never explained. They are simply owned by households from which they, like labor, capital, and entrepreneurial skills, can be sold to business. In the words of Julian Simon, "As economists or consumers, we are interested in the particular services that resources yield, not in the resources themselves." Those services can be provided in many ways and by substituting different factors of production. In Simon's terms, resources can therefore be treated as "infinite."[2]

A second observation is that this model treats economic growth not only as the solution to all social ills but also as boundless. To keep up with population growth, the economy must grow. To provide for a higher standard of living, the economy must grow. To alleviate poverty, hunger, and disease, the economy must grow. The possibility that the economy cannot grow indefinitely is simply not part of this model.

Three points made previously summarize the challenges this model faces now and into the near future. First, a large percentage of the world population today lives in abject poverty. Current economic arrangements do not adequately provide the basic needs of billions of people. The current economic paradigm addresses this problem by promoting further economic growth in the "developing" world. But, the world would require significant economic growth during the next few decades just to meet the basic needs of the poorest of the planet's population. According to some estimates, the global economy would need to grow by a factor of five-to-tenfold over the next 50 years to bring the standard of living of present populations in the developing world into line with the standard of living in the industrialized world.[3]

Second, the world's population during this period will continue to increase significantly, particularly in the most impoverished and already highly populated regions. Even assuming a reduced rate of growth, worldwide population over the next 50 years likely will almost double, to about ten billion people.[4] Thus, economic activity to meet the basic needs of the world's population in the near future will need to increase proportionately.

Additionally, the only sources for all this economic activity are the natural resources of the Earth itself. Many of these resources—clean air, drinkable water, fertile soil, and food—cannot be replaced by the remaining factors of production. We cannot breathe, drink, eat, or grow food on, labor, capital or entrepreneurial skills alone. Because the world's environment is already under stress from current economic activity, the future looks bleak unless major changes take place. Given these realities, we must create an economic system that can provide the needs of the world's population without destroying the environment in the process. This, according to some, is the role of sustainable economics and sustainable development.

Daly argues that neoclassical economics, with its emphasis on economic growth as the goal of economic policy, will inevitably fail to meet these challenges unless it recognizes that the economy is but a subsystem within Earth's biosphere. Economic activity takes place within this biosphere and cannot expand beyond its capacity to sustain life. All the factors that go into production—natural resources, capital, entrepreneurial skills, and labor—ultimately originate in the productive capacity of the Earth. In light of this, the entire classic model will prove unstable if resources move through this system at a rate that outpaces the productive capacity of the Earth or of the Earth's capacity to absorb the wastes and byproducts of this production. Thus, we need to develop an economic system that uses resources only at a rate that can be sustained over the long term and that recycles or reuses both the byproducts of the production process and the products themselves. A model of such a system, based on the work of Daly, is illustrated in Figure B.[5]

Figure B differs from Figure A in several important ways. First, there is a recognition that the economy exists within a finite biosphere that encompasses little more than a few miles-wide ban surrounding the Earth's surface. From the first law of thermodynamics (the conservation of matter/energy), we recognize that neither matter nor energy can truly be "created," it can only be transferred from one form to another. Second, energy is lost at every stage of economic activity. Consistent with the second law of thermodynamics (entropy increased within a closed system), the amount of usable energy decreases over time. "Waste energy" leaves the economic system continuously, and thus new low entropy energy must constantly flow into the system. Ultimately, the only source for new usable energy is the sun. Third, natural resources are no longer

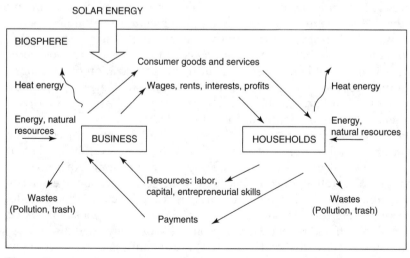

Figure B

treated as undifferentiated and unexplained factors of production emerging from households. Natural resource come from the biosphere and cannot be created *ex nihilo*. Finally, wastes are produced at each stage of economic activity, and these wastes are dumped back into the biosphere.

The conclusion that should be drawn from this new model is relatively simple. Over the long term, resources and energy cannot be used, nor wastes produced, at rates at which the biosphere cannot replace or absorb them without jeopardizing its ability to sustain (human) life. These are what Daly calls the "biophysical limits to growth."[6] The biosphere can produce resources indefinitely, and it can absorb wastes indefinitely, but only at a certain rate and with a certain type of economic activity. This is the goal of sustainable development. Finding this rate and type of economic activity, creating a sustainable business practice, is the ultimate environmental responsibility of business.

Figure B also provides us with a model for interpreting the major environmental policy areas. The consensus for eliminating pollution and wastes, for prudent use of resources, for preserving environmentally sensitive areas and biodiversity can be understood as requiring economic institutions to operate in a sustainable manner within the biosphere.

THE ETHICS OF THE CONVENTIONAL MODEL

Chapter Three suggested that the standard model, in both its economic and corporate social responsibility (CSR) levels, seems to reflect standard utilitarian and Kantian ethical theories. Economic growth and the corresponding managerial goal of profits are thought to serve the utilitarian purpose of maximizing overall happiness. More goods and services in the economy mean that people have more resources with which to satisfy their desires. Getting what they desire, in turn, increases happiness. When business managers pursue profits, they ensure that goods and services get to those individuals who most value them, thus ensuring an optimization of happiness. The Kantian component of this standard model establishes a principled limitation on this utilitarian objective: increase happiness as long as individual rights, or the moral minimum, are not violated.

However, despite appearances, this standard model cannot appeal to the ethics of utilitarianism in its defense. In fact, a strong case can be made that economic growth is ethically vacuous. Despite the appearance that markets are committed to utilitarian ends, in actuality the goal of economic efficiency lacks any coherent and substantive ethical basis at all. The conventional model offers prescriptions for both public policy and managerial responsibility based on the analyses offered by neoclassical economics. But why should society or managers follow this advice? The answer, presumably, is because doing so will lead us to a better state of affairs. At first glance, this better state of affairs—economic efficiency—appears to be the utilitarian goal of providing the greatest good for the greatest number. But does economic efficiency provide the greatest good for the greatest number? Philosopher Mark Sagoff is persuasive in claiming that it does not.[7]

What is the goal of economic efficiency? Efficiency implies optimal satisfaction of consumer preferences. An efficient market is one in which more people get more of that for which they are most willing to pay. But why should anyone take the satisfaction of individual preferences as our overriding goal? Why should this be the goal of public policy when we recognize the obvious and acknowledge that some individual preferences are silly, foolish, vulgar, dangerous, immoral, criminal, and the like? Why should we think that satisfying the preferences of a racist, a criminal, a fool, or a sadist is a good thing? To claim that there is a market for some "good" is simply to say that someone is willing to pay something for it. Efficient markets work to provide an optimal satisfaction of such "goods." But, when we recognize that people are willing to pay for many ethically questionable goods and services, the ethical legitimacy of markets becomes an open question.

What exactly is so good about satisfying preferences? The only possible answers are that satisfying preferences is either a good in itself or that it is a means to something that is good in itself. Given the wide variety of harmful, decadent, and trivial preferences that exist, surely no one could claim that satisfying preferences is good in itself. Surely it is not good in itself that child molesters or rapists have their preferences satisfied. If not good in itself, then the only possible reason for satisfying preferences is that doing so is instrumentally valued for producing something else that is good in itself. But what other good is brought about instrumentally by satisfying preferences?

Typically, this economic approach uses such terms as *utility, welfare, well-being,* or *happiness* to explain the result of satisfying preferences. Public policy should promote economic efficiency and economic growth, and business management ought to pursue profit by satisfying consumer demand, because doing so will result in optimizing utility, welfare, well-being, or happiness.

Let us take this claim empirically and ask what evidence exists to support it. Is it true that the satisfaction of consumer demand, and the economic growth that accompanies it, brings about greater well-being or happiness? It turns out that there is a great deal of evidence to suggest that this is very often false. Happiness is not always correlated with increased wealth and consumer satisfaction. Satisfying my preference for a cigarette, for example, does not always make me happy. Conversely, sometimes having my preferences frustrated can be in my best interest by teaching me patience, diligence, or modesty. Sometimes satisfying preferences is disappointing. Sometimes I might have all that the market can supply, but I might still lack what is important ("What good does it benefit a man if he gains a kingdom but loses his soul?").[8]

But economists might point out that interpreting the relation between satisfied preferences and happiness as an empirical question misunderstands the nature of economics. Economics is not making an empirical claim about preferences and happiness, economics *defines* happiness or welfare or well-being as the satisfaction of preferences. What economists *mean* by happiness is simply that people get what they want.

However, to explain the value of preference satisfaction by simply defining it in these ways is to beg the question by offering a trivially true explanation. Remember how this issue arose. The dominant economic and managerial paradigm offers prescription for what public policy ought to do. When asked for a justification for these prescriptions, we are answered that such policies will produce an optimal satisfaction of consumer preferences. When asked why we should seek this, in light of the trivial and immoral preferences that some people have, we are told that satisfying preferences produces happiness. But when it is explained that this seems empirically false, the answer is that satisfying preferences and happiness *mean* the same thing. But now the argument has come full circle. Why should we adopt a policy aimed to optimally satisfy preferences? Because optimal satisfying preferences results in the optimal satisfaction of preferences. The circular reasoning is a *reduction ad absurdum* of the ethical basis of neoclassical economics.

Thus, even if (and it is a big *if*) economic analysis could overcome all the problems associated with applying market analyses to the real world, and the market succeeded in attaining its goal, we still would have no ethical reason for accepting preference satisfaction as an ethical goal. An efficient allocation of resources is not itself an ethical goal at all.

The final ethical defense of this model of corporate social responsibility reflects a duty-based ethics rather than a utilitarian ethics. This view argues that only the duties to obey the law and refrain from causing harm can legitimately restrict business' pursuit of profit. This view holds that business has only the negative environmental duty to cause no harm but no positive duty to do good or prevent harm.

Traditionally, there are two general rationales offered in defense of this ethical conclusion: Positive duties would violate the respect owed to each individual as an autonomous agent, and there are no rationally defensible or widely acknowledged positive goods that can be binding on individuals. I contend that in the case of business's environmental responsibilities, neither of these two rationales is persuasive.

Let us consider the autonomy side first. Philosophical liberals argue that only negative duties prohibiting harm are compatible with the respect owed to an individual as a free and autonomous agent. Requiring an agent to perform positive acts of goodness is to treat that agent as a means to an end, to coerce that agent against her will, and to have one's ends chosen by another. Thus, the moral respect owed to individuals trumps the goods that can be attained through positive duties.

However, this is to forget the obvious: Business institutions are not moral agents who have an overriding right to be treated with the respect due to autonomous individuals. Business institutions are not autonomous individuals; they are precisely the type of thing Kant had in mind when he spoke of means, rather than ends. Thus, requiring business to serve human ends is to treat business exactly in accord with its nature as a human institution designed and created to serve human ends. Human beings, acting in concert through their social, political, and legal institutions, created the modern corporation and established its legal and ethical duties. My proposal is simply that those duties need to be rethought.

That leaves only the value-relativist claim standing opposed to my proposal. This response claims that we cannot expect business to be responsible for achieving social goods because society itself lacks any consensus on the nature of the good. In the terms of traditional liberalism, the right has priority over the good because of irreconcilable disagreements over the nature of the good. Who is to say what is, or is not, good?

The converse of this view, the priority of the good over the right, is highly contentious in recent ethics. Nevertheless, I would like to defend something very much like it in this book. If we could offer a rationally defensible account of the good for business, one objectively better than the value-neutral model of business that emerges from neoclassical economics, the final rationale for granting business wide freedom in its pursuit of profit disappears. I believe that the goods—ethical, economic, and environmental—that constitute the goals of sustainability offer just such a rationally defensible account of the good.

SUMMARY AND CONCLUSIONS

Market failures are an inescapable fact of economic life. When the costs of market failure are as irreversible and permanent as global climate change and species extinction, we have strong reasons not to trust the market. Consumer demand can play an adequate role in setting policy only if that demand is free from outside influence and only if every affected consumer can express his or her desires in the market. The dominant role of marketing in contemporary business, and the inability of future generations to participate in the market, give us good reasons not to trust consumer demand. Additionally, government regulation has a role to play in directing policy toward sustainability, but like markets and consumers, government action may occur too late or too slowly to prevent irreversible harm, and may be inappropriately influenced by business lobbying.

To raise doubts about market-based and consumer-driven approaches to sustainability is not to suggest that markets and consumers do not have a role or a responsibility to play. The environmental pragmatism introduced in Chapter Two encourages multiple strategies to addressing these challenges. The conclusion is that reliance on the market and consumer demand, even if supplemented by government regulation, will be an insufficient basis for developing sound sustainable business practices.

An economically and ethically adequate role for business will involve responding to consumer demand as expressed in markets, as well as obedience to government regulation. But sustainable business ethics also requires leadership from business. Executives, stockholders, and employees must seize some of the initiative and take responsibility for bringing about the transition to a sustainable world. Rather than passively responding to changing environmental, social, and economic circumstances, responsible businesses must take the lead in helping to create a sustainable economy.

Endnotes

1 Versions of the circular flow model presented here can be found in many standard economic textbooks. The model in which the economy is embedded within the biosphere is based on the work of Herman Daly. See, for example, *Beyond Growth* (Boston: Beacon Press, 1996) pp. 47–49.

2 Julian Simon, The Ultimate Resource (Princeton, NJ: Princeton University Press 1981)

3 See, for example, J. MacNeill, "Strategies for Sustainable Development," *Scientific American* 1989, pp. 155–65.

4 For example, Stuart Hart in *Capitalism at the Crossroads* (Upper Saddle River, NJ: Wharton School Publishing, 2005) suggests a stabilization of the world's population at between 8 and 10 billion by mid-century (p. 32).

5 This particular version of this model was developed in my own class at St. John's University during a visit by Professor Daly in 1998.

6 Daly, *Beyond Growth*, 1996, pp. 33–35.

7 Mark Sagoff, *Economy of the Earth* (New York: Cambridge University Press, 1990).

8 Ample empirical evidence suggests an uncertain relationship between happiness and the satisfaction of consumer preferences. See, for example, Juliet Schor, *The Overworked American* (New York, Basic Books, 1991); Benjamin Hunnicutt, *Work Without End: Abandoning Shorter Hours for the Right to Work* (Philadelphia, Temple University Press, 1988), Stanley Lebergott, *Pursuing Happiness: American Consumers in the Twentieth Century* (Princeton, Princeton University Press 1993), and the classic David Riesman, *The Lonely Crowd* (New Haven, Yale University Press, 1969).

chapter five

Ecological Economics and Sustainable Business Ethics

INTRODUCTION

In previous chapters, the dominant model of economics and business was described, and reasons that this paradigm is inadequate to address real economic, environmental, and ethical challenges of the twenty-first century are suggested. In this chapter, I describe an emerging approach to economics that can provide an alternative conceptual framework for understanding sustainable business. I also offer a preliminary sketch of an alternative model of corporate social responsibility that is compatible with ecological economics.

The dominant model of economics and business encourages us to understand the goals of financial profit and environmental responsibility as a conflicting dualism. Managers must choose between profit and social responsibility, between their financial duties to their business and environmental or ethical duties. Cast in these terms, it becomes easy for business leaders to dismiss environmental responsibility. Pursuing environmental goals beyond those required by law or minimal moral duties threatens profit, and profit is necessary to remain in operation; therefore, asking business to pursue environmental goals is unreasonably asking business to jeopardize its very existence. Philosopher Norman Bowie, in an essay mentioned previously, comes very close to accepting this argument when he cites the "ought implies can" principle: ethics cannot claim that business *ought* to do what it *cannot* do without losing profitability.

But this narrow view of corporate responsibility is misguided. Profitability is a necessary condition for a business to exist, but it is not the purpose of business. Models of corporate social responsibility that take profit as the purpose of business have confused means with ends. Theodore Levitt, a leading business and marketing scholar, suggested an alternative model decades ago:

> "The purpose of a business is to create and keep a customer. To do that you have to produce and deliver goods and services that people want and value at a price and under conditions that are reasonably attractive relative to those

offered by others . . . . It was not so long ago that a lot of companies assumed something quite different about the purpose of business. They said quite simply that the purpose is to make money. But that is as vacuous as to say that the purpose of life is to eat. Eating is a prerequisite, not a purpose of life . . . Profits can be made in lots of devious and transient ways. For people of affairs, a statement of purpose should provide guidance to the management of their affairs. To say that they should attract and hold customers forces facing the necessity of figuring out what people really want and value, and then catering to those wants and values. It provides specific guidance, and has moral merit."[1]

As Levitt suggests, there can be many different ways to make a profit, a point that the model of corporate social responsibility associated with neoclassical economics tends to overlook. The challenge for sustainable business management is to pursue profit in ways that contribute to, rather than threaten, ecological sustainability. Sustainability as the purpose of business provides guidance that creative and entrepreneurial business leaders can follow. But if the critical analysis of the previous chapter is correct, business managers cannot look to traditional neoclassical economics for guidance in this. The growth assumption of that economic theory is guaranteed to point in the wrong direction. What is needed is an alternative model of economics that can provide a framework for understanding the responsibilities of the firm within a sustainable society. Ecological economics provides such a framework.

ECOLOGICAL ECONOMICS

Ecological economics, or what is also sometimes called *sustainable economics*, is an emerging field that seeks to integrate economics and ecology.[2] As a definition, one book suggests simply that "ecological economics studies how ecosystems and economic activity inter-relate."[3] Another book rejects any attempt to define the field of ecological economics in terms of some unique body of knowledge or methodology. Instead, the field is understood as a multidisciplinary approach to a particular set of questions.[4] These questions arise in the area where ecology and economics overlap. In that way, ecological economics is less an alternative to neoclassical economics than it is a broader, multidisciplinary approach to a range of problems at the intersection of ecology and economics.

Diagram *B* on page 57 provides a helpful model for thinking about the range of questions addressed by the field of ecological economics. In this diagram, economics is understood as a subset within the wider ecological biosphere. That biosphere is the source for the resources that enter into the economy, and the destination for the wastes and byproducts of that economy. Because that biosphere is the ultimate environment on which all life depends, what the economy takes from and puts into that biosphere must be closely monitored. Thus, the ultimate challenge for the field of ecological economics is to articulate the economic principles that would maintain a vibrant economy within the biophysical limits established by the biosphere. In short, the economic subsystem within the biosphere cannot grow so large that it overshoots the ability of the greater biosphere to support it.

That diagram also suggests that there are three basic categories of these questions: questions concerning the flow of resources into the economy; questions concerning the flow of wastes out of the economy; and questions concerning appropriate and best practices for transforming resources into products and services. There are, therefore, three fundamental challenges for a sustainable economy. First, we must design economic institutions and practices so that the resources that flow into the economic subsystem from the biosphere are not depleted at unsustainable rates. Second, we must design institutions and practices that do not produce wastes flowing out of the economic subsystem at rates at which the biosphere cannot absorb. Third, within the economic subsystem itself we must design institutions and practices that meet the needs of the present generation efficiently and justly without also jeopardizing the well-being of future generations.

Viewed in this way, the goal of ecological economics is to help create an economy that is sufficiently robust to address the real needs of an increasing population, but which does not grow so big that it overshoots the carrying capacity of the biosphere. This is the core idea of sustainable economics: an economy that can continue as a vibrant and productive force into the indefinite future. In the words of one observer, "if 'sustainability' is anything more than a slogan or expression of emotion, it must amount to an injunction to preserve the productive capacity for the indefinite future."[5]

Besides sustainability, several other concepts and metaphors have been used to explain ecological economics. One of the earliest and best-known models was described by economist Kenneth Boulding in 1966 when he suggested the metaphor of "spaceship Earth."[6] Boulding described the growth-based model as "frontier economics," in which vast and infinite resources are assumed to exist right over the horizon. Instead, Boulding suggested that we think of the Earth in terms of a spaceship that must rely on the supplies that it has brought along and, ultimately, solar power for all its needs. (To make the metaphor more accurate, the passengers also are unable to dispose of wastes out into space.) Growing beyond the boundary of a spaceship will prove disastrous. Ecological economics would be like the principles one would adopt to govern the management of a spaceship.

Economist Herman Daly has used the idea of a "steady-state" economy to explain the goal of ecological economics. Daly talks in terms of *throughput*, the combination of matter and energy (which the first law of thermodynamics informs us are ultimately interchangeable) that moves through the economic subsystem of the biosphere. The biosphere establishes the biophysical limits to the physical scale of that throughput; the limits to economic growth.

A *steady-state economy* holds the size of the aggregate throughput constant and seeks a qualitative improvement in the uses made of the matter and energy throughput. This would be *sustainable development* in its only meaningful sense—economic activity that improves the quality of life while remaining on a scale that can be maintained indefinitely.[7] According to Daly, *sustainable growth* is an oxymoron; nothing can continue to grow indefinitely. The goal of economics should be *sustainable development*; the economy can continue to improve and become qualitatively better indefinitely.

This concept of an appropriate *scale* for the aggregate economy is perhaps the central idea of sustainable economics. *An Introduction to Ecological Economics*, a book co-authored by several of its most influential practitioners, explains this point as follows.

> "We see three basic problems: allocation, distribution, and scale. Neoclassical economics deals extensively with allocation, secondarily with distribution, and not at all with scale. Ecological economics deals with all three, and accepts much of neoclassical theory regarding allocation. Our emphasis on the scale question is made necessary by its neglect in standard economics. Inclusion of scale is the biggest difference between ecological economics and neoclassical economics."[8]

If we think of economics as dealing with issues of production and distribution, as many of us have been taught for years, we recognize that the reigning paradigm focuses exclusively on questions of allocation and distribution. Allocation is concerned with the determination of where resources go in the production of goods and services. Allocation addresses the question of *what gets produced* from the resources that enter the economy. Neoclassical economics argues that the price established by the law of supply and demand is the most appropriate means for making this determination. The criterion by which we judge a good allocation is *efficiency*. Labor, capital, and natural resources should be allocated to their most efficient use, that is, the use that would bring about greater overall satisfaction. As we saw in the previous chapter, neoclassical economists believe that relative price is an efficient mechanism for solving most environmental challenges because it achieves an efficient allocation of scarce resources.

Distribution refers to the dispersal of the goods and services produced; addressing the question of *who gets what is produced*. The criterion for judging distribution is an ethical one. Economic goods and services should be distributed according to principles of justice. Some conservative defenders of neoclassical economics argue that a just distribution is whatever results from free exchanges within open and competitive markets. More mainstream interpreters argue that justice demands a fair and equal opportunity to participate in the economy as well as at least a basic minimum guaranteed through tax and welfare policies. Thus, questions of distribution are not exclusively economic questions, but involve ethics, justice, and public policy as well. Although we might rely on price to answer questions of allocation, we rely on political mechanisms and public policy to resolve the distributive questions of social justice.

Ecological economics adds *scale* as a third area for economic consideration. "Scale refers to the physical volume of the throughput, the flow of matter-energy from the environment as low-entropy raw materials and back to the environment as high-entropy wastes."[9] Scales addresses two of the fundamental questions suggested by the model on page 57 what is the rate at which resources move from the biosphere into the economy, and what is the rate at which wastes are dumped back into the biosphere from the economy? The goal would be to attain and maintain an optimal scale for the economy. The criteria for judging optimal scale ultimately would involve all three sustainability measures: economic, ethical, and ecological. An optimal scale would be robust enough economic activity that the real needs of the present global population are being met without subverting the biosphere's ability to provide the resources and absorb the wastes of that economic activity.

Ecological economists often refer to entropy, the Second Law of Thermodynamics, in explicating their approach. Although the topic is complex, and although much controversy surrounds the use of entropy in economics, it can be a useful heuristic device as we think about some of the directions in which a sustainable economy might move. Entropy is the tendency for all energy to disperse, spread out, and, therefore, to become less useful. All energy tends to spread out from concentrated forms in which it can do work, to less and less concentrated forms in which it is incapable of doing work. One implication is that in a closed system, all useful energy will eventually become so dispersed that the system essentially dies. Another implication is that creating more highly concentrated forms of energy can be done within closed systems, but only for the short term and only with the expansion of other sources of energy.

The application of entropy to economics is most closely associated with the twentieth century mathematician and economist Nicholas Georgescu-Roegen.[10] In *The Entropy Law and the Economic Process*, Georgescu-Roegen presented his case that economic activity uses low-entropy energy available in raw materials and transforms it into useful products and services. The entire process will inevitably degrade the amount of useful energy available. Economic activity cannot create new forms of productive matter or energy; it can only use available matter and energy in a way that inevitably converts it into less useful forms.

Georgescu-Roegen proposed an analogy with an hourglass to explain the significance of entropy to economics. The sands of an hourglass exist in a closed system, with no sand entering or leaving. The amount of sand is constant, it can neither be created nor destroyed. Sand in the upper chamber is in a low-entropy highly concentrated form ready to do work. The energy is expanded, and it is available for doing work, by falling down into the lower chamber. Once it is in the bottom, it is dispersed into a high-entropy state and no longer available to do work.

Georgescu-Roegen's introduction of the concept of entropy from physics into economics has been very controversial. For example, neither the economy nor the Earth's biosphere is a closed system, and, therefore, the application of entropy to economics is inexact. But there is a lesson to be learned from this. If we do treat the biosphere as a closed system, using only the low-entropy energy that is readily available in the Earth's stock of resources, we will inevitably be degrading the matter and energy available for economic use. If we emphasize the open-system aspects of the biosphere in our economic activity, particularly if we recognize the sun as the source of any new energy coming into the system, we have the potential to transform an otherwise deteriorating process into something more stable and lasting.

POLICY IMPLICATIONS OF ECOLOGICAL ECONOMICS: ACCOUNTING FOR NATURAL CAPITAL

Much of the work being done within ecological economics has focused on the theory-building stage of this new discipline, seeking to articulate the theoretical model for an ecological economics. Much other work has been done at the macroeconomic level, defending prescriptions for international and national economic policy based on the principles of ecological economics. In many ways, in this book attempts are made to draw out the implications a step further, examining the implications of ecological economics to business firms. Before turning to that task, however, it will prove useful to consider some of the macroeconomic implications drawn from the principles of ecological economics.

Because the problems associated with finding an appropriate scale for the economic subsystem within the Earth's biosphere are truly global, much of the attention has been directed at institutions that can influence global economic development. Organizations such as the World Bank, the International Monetary Fund, have been particularly encouraged to adopt policies that would foster sustainable development.

Many policy recommendations are concerned with how natural capital should be accounted for and treated within the global economy. Generally, ecological economics argues that natural resources should be treated as capital, not income. That is, we must recognize, and act on the recognition, that the biosphere is capable of producing goods and services on which we rely. In general, *capital* typically refers to those manufactured resources that, along with land and labor, are the basic factors of production. Fixed capital refers to manufactured resources such as buildings, equipment, machinery, and technology. Working capital refers to the stocks or parts on hand that are available for immediate production. Economists also refer to financial capital, which refers to those funds that are available to operate a business.

Capital can be used to in two fundamentally different ways. Well-managed capital produces a steady-stream of income without depleting the store of capital. This occurs, for example, when money is invested and earns interest or dividends. Good investments return interest payments indefinitely. But capital also can be productive when it is sold-off. If I sell my machinery or spend my savings, my capital has not produced an income as much as it has been liquidated. In fact, the classic definition of income is "the maximum amount that a community can consume over some time period and still be as well off at the end of the period as at the beginning."[11] Prudent business operations, therefore, invest in capital so that it might produce a steady income. The classic fable of the goose that laid the golden eggs is a lesson about what happens when one confuses capital with income.

Ecological economics argues that natural resources too often are treated as income rather than as capital. In the past, economics has looked at the store of natural resources available to a country or industry as if it were a free and inexhaustible income. Modern economies have been liquidating their savings to support their present lifestyles. If, instead, we come to understand natural resources as capital rather than income, then future policy can be inferred from fairly standard economic principles. If natural resources are part of the capital stock from which income is generated, and if the supply of that capital is dwindling, as current environmental trends suggest, prudent economic policy would require that we (1) seek ways to increase the productivity of that capital, and (2) invest in increasing the supply of natural capital.[12]

Consider how such thinking might be applied in agriculture. To be productive, a farm requires a variety of capital resources: tractors, seed, irrigation pipes, and so forth. It also needs labor and land. A farm can only be as productive as allowed by the least productive of these factors, what economists call the limiting factor. All the tractors and seed in the world would be useless without available labor to drive the tractors and plant the seed. A farmer with plentiful labor and abundant seed but no tractor would be well advised to invest in a tractor. A prudent farmer would seek to increase the productivity of the limiting factor. Thus, if labor is the limiting factor, the farmer might work longer hours. A prudent farmer would also invest in this limiting factor by hiring more workers or training them better. If, as often happens during harvest time, machinery is the limiting factor, a prudent farmer might drive his combine through the night, rent an additional combine, or invest by purchasing a new machine. The point is that a prudent person searches for ways to increase the productivity of whichever factor of production is limiting overall production.

Ecological economics argues that natural capital is fast becoming the limiting factor in global economic production; therefore, rational economic policy should shift to increasing the productivity of natural capital over the short term, and invest in natural capital over the longer-term.

Many mainstream economists reject this analysis. As we saw in Chapter Three, some economists argue that the supply of natural resources is effectively infinite. If this is so, natural capital will never be the limiting factor, and economic policy should continue to emphasize investment in traditional capital and labor costs. The outcome of this debate hinges on the question of whether natural and non-natural resources are substitutes. Traditional economists such as Julian Simon argue that they are. Ecological economists argue that they are not.

Simon's argument asserts that the issue is not really about "resources" in the sense of physical objects, but about resources in the sense of the services supplied to humans from those objects. Therefore, although the amount of copper in the Earth's crust is finite, the supply of transmission lines for electricity and phones or plumbing pipes is not. People value copper not in itself, but for the services it supplies. As the physical supply of copper limits the production of those services, entrepreneurial individuals will create other means for supplying those services. Thus, the supply of entrepreneurial labor or capital investment can be substituted for the apparently short supply of natural resources. Therefore, economic activity can remain sustainable as long as the total amount of all resources—labor (including entrepreneurial skills), natural resources, capital—does not shrink. Because human creativity and labor, at least, will exist as long as there are humans around, economic growth is sustainable. This view is often referred to as the *weak sustainability thesis*.

Ecological economists argue that natural resources and the other factors of production are complements rather than substitutes. That is, each is needed in production and substitution of one for the other is limited. This view is often referred to as the *strong sustainability thesis* because it holds that an economy is sustainable only if the supply of natural resources is not depleted beyond a certain point. As Herman Daly points out, "The complementarity of man-made and natural capital is made obvious at a concrete and common-sense level by asking, What good is a sawmill without a forest, a fishing boat without populations of fish, a refinery without petroleum deposits, an irrigated farm without an aquifer or river? We have long recognized the complementarity between public infrastructure and private capital—what good is a car or truck without roads to drive on?"[13]

Treating natural resources as capital rather than as income also suggests changes in national and international accounting practices. Treating as healthy a national economy that spends down its supply of natural resources is, like any practice that treats wealth as income, misguided. Over the short term such an economy can appear to grow, as a person who spends his life savings appears to be rich. But over the long term, this is a recipe for economic disaster.

The differences between accounting for growth and accounting for development have also encouraged ecological economists to develop economic measures that would be alternatives to Gross Domestic Product (GDP) and other traditional aggregate measures of economic activity. GDP is the most common indicator of economic well-being within a country. GDP is measured in terms of dollars. The assumption is that we seek a measure of overall well-being within a society and, because the price of goods is an accurate measure of their value, we can measure the present well-being of a society by measuring how much it spends. Individual happiness is equated with getting what one wants; what one is willing to pay most for is equated with what one most wants; therefore, the more people spend, the happier we can assume they are. By measuring spending, we measure the aggregate level of a society's happiness.

Understood in this way, we recognize that GDP does not measure such factors as health, infant mortality, illiteracy, environmental destruction, ecological decay, topsoil productivity, groundwater and aquifer reserves, CO_2 emissions, the accumulation of toxic chemicals in breast milk or food, loss of habitat, species extinction, psychological well-being, peace, or discrimination. Thus, ecological economists (as well as many others) seek to develop measures that provide a more accurate portrait of a society's ecological, social, and ethical health.

One such model is the Genuine Progress Indicator (GPI).[14] Developed by the Redefining Progress organization, the GPI is an attempt to provide a positive measure for such beneficial factors as family health, leisure time, community involvement and volunteerism, household work, parenting, and resource productivity. Economic spending that is done to mitigate the loss of such things is subtracted from rather than added to the economic measure of a society's well-being. Thus, money spent as a result of family breakdowns, crime, disease, pollution, auto accidents, and other harmful activities count against rather than for a society's welfare. As part of their work, the Redefining Progress group has developed the "ecological footprint" measure of each individual's impact on the Earth's ecosystems.[15] The United Nations also has worked to develop an alternative measure. The United Nations Human Development Index (UNHDI) attempts to measure such things as life expectancy, literacy, purchasing power, gender and racial equity, and educational opportunities.

Moving from this macrolevel, comparable sustainability measures are being developed by many individual firms, trade organizations, and nongovernmental organizations (NGOs). For example, the Global Reporting Initiative (GRI) is an independent NGO that develops and disseminates globally applicable Sustainability Reporting Guidelines (SRI). These guidelines help individual firms develop an assessment of their own economic, environmental, and social dimensions of their activities, products, and services. GRIs are voluntary reports that function much like standard annual financial reports. The GRI works in cooperation with UN Secretary-General Kofi Annan's Global Compact and the United Nations Environment Programme (UNEP).[16]

POLICY IMPLICATIONS OF ECOLOGICAL ECONOMICS: GLOBALIZED TRADE AND FINANCE

Two other policy implications of ecological economics that are relevant for business practice have drawn attention in this literature. First, ecological economics is less sanguine than neoclassical economics about the benefits of free trade on a global scale. Increasing global economic integration, without a conscious focus on sustainability, raises serious ecological and ethical concerns. Second, the emphasis on scale inclines ecological economists to support microfinance programs to encourage and support indigenous people in creating local businesses enterprises.

The conventional model tends to support investment in giant infrastructure projects with the belief that there is a single and universal strategy for economic development. Sustainable economics, in deference to the particularities of culture, geography, and history, is more sympathetic to development projects and economic activities that are time and place specific. Microfinancing initiatives, in addition to major national investment projects, are one way to support economic development that is sensitive to localized situations.

Two decades ago, the topic of global free trade and globalization was discussed almost exclusively in the disciplines of political science and international relations. Today, it is an essential component of business, management, and ethics. Whereas two decades ago, nation-states were the prime movers of international trade, today transnational corporations (TNCs) have more influence over international trade and finance than many nation-states. The ethical implications of this evolution, especially in the areas of workers' rights and the environment, have been enormous.

Globalization refers to a process of international economic integration. Although international trade and cooperation have existed for as long as there have been nations, this process of international economic integration has become increasingly more common, and its pace has accelerated in just the past decade or two. Compared to the 1980s, today's world is characterized by increased trade, freer trade, faster and freer flow of capital and information, and increased consolidation of market power in the hands of TNCs.

International trade agreements such as the General Agreement on Tariffs and Trade (GATT) and the North American Free Trade Agreement

(NAFTA) opened borders to freer trade. The continuing growth of and integration within the European Union, including the adoption of a single currency (the "Euro") beginning in 2002, has turned Europe into what is essentially a single economy. International loans from the World Bank have supported major development projects throughout the world. Monetary policies established by the IMF have made it increasingly easy for capital to flow between countries. Perhaps less slowly, immigration policies are making the international flow of people and labor easier. The worldwide effects of recent economic recessions in Japan and the United States, along with currency devaluations in Mexico and Argentina, testify to how interdependent the world's economies truly are.

The neoclassical model of economics includes a strong and principled support for free trade. The ethical case for free trade and international economic cooperation implicit within that model has been widely accepted by governments, industry, and economists. The major argument in favor is a more generalized version of the market argument we examined in Chapters Three and Four. The pursuit of profit within social and economic arrangements that secure free and open competition will allocate resources to their most highly valued uses and distribute those resources in ways that will produce the greatest good for the greatest number of people. The pursuit of profit through efficiencies will lead to specialization through the comparative advantages different countries and different regions enjoy. Globalization is the process of extending this free and open competition beyond national borders. International competition for labor, jobs, goods and services, natural resources, and capital will, over time, increase the overall well-being of everyone.

This view has two implications that are central to sustainable development. First, the economic growth and development that flows from more free and open trade is thought to be the most effective way to improve the well-being of the most impoverished people in the world. International economic integration, according to defenders of globalization, is an essential step in worldwide economic growth, and only this growth can adequately address worldwide poverty and deprivation. Second, defenders of this process argue that economic integration is a major impediment to conflict. The more countries cooperate economically, the less likely they will be to fight militarily. Thus, globalization is seen as a major step in reducing both poverty and the possibility of war.[17]

Critics raise two challenges to increasing globalization that are relevant to our purposes here. First, some critics charge that globalization leads to more poverty and less freedom for the world's poor. Second, many environmentalists and labor supporters argue that free global markets will encourage a "race to the bottom" of environmental and labor standards. Thus, the economic debates about the effects of free global trade and the other policies of increased global economic integration are central to sustainable development. If markets function as defenders of the neoclassical model believe, the path to sustainable development includes freer world markets and trade. If the effects of poverty increase, and environmental health and working conditions deteriorate, freer global trade is unsustainable.

In a recent book, economist Jeffrey Sachs outlines proposals to end extreme poverty by 2025.[18] Sachs's proposals rely heavily on free market mechanisms, and he is critical of skeptics of globalization. "By now the anti-globalization movement should see that globalization, more than anything else, has reduced the numbers of extreme poor in India by two hundred million and in China by three hundred million since 1990."[19]

Let us assume that Sachs is correct and that the economic development that has taken place in India and China over the past two decades has decreased the number of their citizens living in extreme poverty. Let us also assume that, as a matter of fact, freer trade and freer markets have been instrumental in bringing this about. Does this mean that the conventional model of economic growth is the most rational path to sustainable development? Does this mean that business leaders need only pursue profits and allow the invisible hand of the market to direct economic activity to socially responsible ends? Several factors suggest that it does not mean this at all.

Economic growth in India and China in recent years has been impressive. But it is also the case that similar programs adopting conventional economic wisdom have not brought about comparable economic improvement in Africa. In fact, massive international economic aid and incentives have a much longer history in Africa than in India and China. So, what explains apparent success in India and China and lack of success in Africa? Two answers are common in the literature.

First, many observers believe that African countries have lacked the political and social stability necessary for economic development. Wars, oppression, and corruption have prevented many African countries from following the conventional path toward development. Furthermore, many modern African countries were carved out of colonial empires in the past century, and their borders bear little relationship to much deeper cultural and social realities. Thus, according to this view, healthy market economies have not yet had a chance to develop throughout much of Africa.

A second answer discounts the explanatory power of political and social instability. "Africa's governance is poor because Africa is poor," according to Sachs; not the other way around. After all, until recently, China has had a very repressive and undemocratic government, yet it has been welcoming to market freedoms and economic growth. This second perspective (and one to which Sachs seems attracted) argues that the particular geographical factors play a significant role in economic development. Access to transportation, especially access to the sea; natural resources available for export; drought; lack of fertile soil; lack of energy sources; tropical climates; and disease, have all played a significant role in the inability of African countries to follow the market path to development.

But, notice what this very debate seems to entail. The prescriptions of market economics alone are not enough to guarantee economic development without some degree of both social-political and environmental support. This seems to be a recognition of the very lesson of sustainable economics: long-term sustainable development must address all three pillars of sustainability: economic, environmental, and ethical. As described previously, ecological economics is not an alternative to the neoclassical model; it seeks to supplement it with ecological (and ethical) considerations. Rather than offer a blanket endorsement of neoclassical policies, ecological economics would encourage a broader approach that takes into consideration the environmental, social, and political realities of each specific situation. Interestingly, this is not unlike the conclusion Sachs himself arrives at in defending what he calls "clinical economics."[20] The lesson seems to be that economic development cannot be passively left to the workings of market mechanisms, but must be guided by an active and conscious awareness of environmental and ethical factors.

Two additional considerations cast doubt on the adequacy of a strict reliance on market mechanisms to foster international development. First, the neoclassical approach remains utilitarian at its center. The goal is the overall, or collective, welfare of a society. Poverty is decreased when the overall GDP and per capita income increase. But this collective approach fails to address the distributive question: who benefits and who suffers from such economic growth? Secondly, even if there is evidence to suggest that market mechanisms can play a primary role in the economic development of some countries and regions, it does not follow that it can play a similar role for all countries and regions. Let us consider each of these concerns in turn.

To say that the neoclassical model is fundamentally utilitarian is to emphasize its collective aspects. Utilitarian justice, and its economic twin efficiency, is understood in terms of *overall* benefits and *greatest number* of beneficiaries. In contrast, ethical traditions that emphasize the inherent dignity of each individual understand justice in terms of such individual rights as equality, fairness, liberty. The deep ethical challenge to utilitarian justice is that beneficial overall benefits should not be sought at the expense of individual rights. The utilitarian ends do not justify the means, if the means involve treating individuals in ways that violate their rights.

Consider how this controversy would play out in the case of exporting dangerous or toxic wastes. The economic case for such exports was made clearly some years ago in a memo from then World Bank chief economist Lawrence Summers.

Date: December 12, 1991

To: Distribution

From: Lawrence H. Summers

Subject: GEP 'Dirty' Industries:

Just between you and me, shouldn't the World Bank be encouraging MORE migration of the dirty industries to the LDCs (Less Developed Countries)? I can think of three reasons:

1. The measurements of the costs of health-impairing pollution depend on the foregone earnings from increased morbidity and mortality. From this point of view a given amount of health impairing pollution should be done in the country with the lowest cost, which will be the country with the lowest wages. I think the economic logic behind dumping a load of toxic waste in the lowest wage country is impeccable and we should face up to that.

2. The costs of pollution are likely to be nonlinear as the initial increments of pollution probably have very low cost. I've always thought that underpopulated countries in Africa are vastly UNDERpolluted; their air quality is probably vastly inefficiently low compared to Los Angeles or Mexico City. Only the lamentable facts that so much pollution is generated by nontradable industries (transport, electrical generation) and that the unit transport costs of solid waste are so high prevent world welfare enhancing trade in air pollution and waste.

3. The demand for a clean environment for aesthetic and health reasons is likely to have very high-income elasticity. The concern over an agent that causes a one in a million change in the odds of prostrate cancer is obviously going to be much higher in a country where people survive to get prostrate cancer than in a country where mortality under 5 is 200 per 1000. Also, much of the concern over industrial atmosphere discharge is about visibility impairing particulates. These discharges may have very little direct health impact. Clearly trade in goods that embody aesthetic pollution concerns could be welfare enhancing. Although production is mobile, the consumption of pretty air is a nontradable. The problem with the arguments against all of these proposals for more pollution in LDCs (intrinsic rights to certain goods, moral reasons, social concerns, lack of adequate markets, etc.) could be turned around and used more or less effectively against every Bank proposal for liberalization.[21]

In short, endangering the health and lives of poor people rather than wealthier individuals whose own consumerism created such toxic wastes would be more efficient and would produce greater good for a greater number of people. Utilitarian and market-based versions of justice conclude that this is fair; most other theories of justice argue that it is decidedly unfair and unjust.

This issue remains relevant more than a decade after Summers' memo. Consider that both the production and disposal of information and communication technology products, especially computers, monitors, and televisions, create significant toxic wastes. For example, it requires 1.8 tons of water, fossil fuels, and chemicals to produce the average desktop computer with a 17-inch CRT monitor. What happens to these products when consumers are done with them and the wastes generated in their production? Santa Clara County in California, home of Silicon Valley, has more Superfund sites (23) than any other county in the United States. (Los Angeles County is second, with 17 Superfund sites.) Between 50 percent and 80 percent of e-wastes collected for recycling in the United States are, in fact, not recycled but are exported to developing countries, with China and India among the leading recipients. It is not unusual for impoverished Chinese and Indian women and children mostly to pick apart these products by hand, sometimes burning the plastic cases, to recover recyclable metals.[22] Again, real questions of justice arise when the dangers associated with the consumer products of industrialized countries products are borne by vulnerable people who are neither responsible for, nor benefit from, those products.

In addition to the justice challenge, this issue also highlights the potential for the problem referred to as the "race to the bottom." There is an economic incentive to send socially undesirable jobs, practices, wastes, and products to the poorest countries and regions. Such countries have great incentive, and little alternative, to accept such imports and are not in a position to impose health, safety, wage, or environmental regulations. Poor countries enjoy their comparative economic advantage in the market for toxic imports and dangerous jobs precisely because they do not impose costly regulations. Because other countries will lose the economic benefits of this market to countries without standards, an incentive is created for countries with standards to lower or eliminate any standards that they have. Thus begins a race to the bottom of health, safety, wage, and environmental regulation. In the world of free trade, such regulations create "non-tariff barriers to trade" and thus are an impediment to economic growth.

A more sustainable approach to economic development recognizes that such harmful ethical and environmental consequences really are market failures on an international level. Like all market failures, they stand in need of government regulation and mandate to ensure that markets function without creating undeserved and uncompensated harms.

Finally, sustainable economics has reservations about the generalizability of market-based paths to development. That is, even if market mechanisms have led to economic growth in some countries, there are good reasons to doubt that these mechanisms can be generalized to every country. Specifically, a good case can be made for concluding that economic growth in industrialized countries throughout the nineteenth and twentieth centuries could occur only because there were large, undeveloped regions with vast amounts of cheap and readily available resources to fuel that growth. Think of how the extensive worldwide colonial systems of the European countries were stimulated and supported by the exploitation of resources from their colonies. Think of how economic growth in the United States has been fueled by inexpensive oil imported from the Middle East.

Thus, the claim is that long-term economic growth has been possible for many countries because of, at least in part, readily available and cheap natural resources supplied by nonindustrial countries. This means that what has worked for some countries is unlikely to work for all. A more sustainable economic model needs to recognize that cheap imports of natural resources will not be capable of stimulating economic development in the future in the way that it has in the past.

A final policy initiative associated with a more sustainable and ecological economic model focuses on the ability of microcredit and microfinancing programs to stimulate local economic development. Microcredit policies extend small loans directly to poor people to finance small business and self-employment opportunities. In this way, the world's poorest people are directly helped to become self-sufficient. In traditional economic and international aid terms, microcredit is truly revolutionary.

Consider the conventional model of international lending, as practiced by such institutions as the World Bank, aims to alleviate poverty. Poverty is a massive problem; therefore, it is assumed that loans directed to ease poverty must be massive. But, of course, the only institution deemed credit-worthy enough to receive such enormous loans is the government. Thus, standard economic thinking about international aid encourages huge loans to governments that are targeted for enormous infrastructure projects such as road construction, dams and water systems, power plants, and industrial development. The conventional economic assumption is that such projects will create the conditions for economic growth and, eventually, jobs and other benefits will trickle down to the country's poorest citizens.

In practice, this approach results in large foreign debts for the world's poorest countries. To repay those debts, countries need to acquire hard currencies, usually American dollars. In turn, this requires an economy focused on exports, primarily to the United States. Thus, the infrastructure created by loans intended to help the poor is targeted at creating an export economy, often centered upon raw materials, agricultural exports, or consumer goods. Only secondarily will such an economy produce the goods and services—food, health care, local jobs, education, housing—that would directly benefit the poorest citizens. Furthermore, this process will involve a centralization of industry and jobs, thus encouraging a migration from the countryside into cities. Often enough, those remaining in the countryside are women and children and are made worse-off than they had been previously because their husbands, fathers, and brothers have left. Those who migrate to the cities are also often made worse-off because there are seldom enough jobs available for all who move and, unlike the countryside, there are fewer opportunities for self-sufficiency in the city.

Even more troubling is the fact that little of the financial aid itself ever reaches the poorest people. For example, one report claims that of $30 billion in foreign aid directed to Bangladesh in the last quarter of the twentieth century, only 25 percent of it was actually spent in Bangladesh. The remaining 75 percent was spent in the donor countries themselves on administrative, equipment, and commodity costs.[23] Because international loans are targeted for huge infrastructure projects, and because the equipment and expertise for such projects exists primarily in the developed world, much of the money ends up in the developed countries. In fact, much of international aid, and especially food aid, come with a requirement that products be purchased from the lending countries. Of the money that actually reached Bangladesh in those years, most of it went to local suppliers, contractors, and others among that country's elite.

Microcredit is one alternative to such enormous international loans. Developed within the last few decades, microcredit policies target loans and financing directly to poor people themselves, enabling the poor to become more self-sufficient. Microcredit extends loans at low interest rates to people for self-employment and entrepreneurial projects that have potential to help people escape poverty and become self-reliant. Traditional lending institutions would not make loans to the poor—the people who most need credit—because poor people are deemed unworthy of credit. They have no resources to use as collateral for a loan. Furthermore, traditional lending institutions judge the amount of money typically involved in microcredit loans, often less than $100, too small to be profitable.

Perhaps the best known microcredit institution is the Grameen Bank of Bangladesh, founded by economist "2006 Nobel Peace Prize winner" Muhammad Yunus.[24] After teaching economics in the United States for many years, Yunus returned to his native Bangladesh in the early 1970s when that country gained its independence from Pakistan. Yunus hoped he could contribute to this new country's independence with his expertise in economics. Bangladesh was a desperately poor country struggling with the effects of a harsh famine. Yunus soon came to believe that the people of Bangladesh needed more direct help than what he offered in a university economics class.

While touring the rural villages one day (the name "Grameen" translates as rural or village in the Bangla language), he met a small group of women who were making bamboo stools that they later sold at local markets. The women explained that they borrowed money from local money-lenders to purchase supplies, sometimes paying as much as 10 percent interest each week. Supplies cost only pennies a day, but after repaying their loans, the women earned 2 cents each day. This amount kept the women and their families in a cycle of poverty, earning just enough to repay debts but never enough to escape debt. After investigating further, Yunus and his students concluded that the entire village was kept in debt by borrowing that amounted to less than $27. The idea for the Grameen Bank was born from the recognition that very small amounts of capital, loaned directly to poor people at low rates, could have a tremendous positive impact in helping entire villages escape a cycle of poverty.

Three decades later, Jeffrey Sachs seems to reach a similar conclusion in his book *The End of Poverty*. Sachs's concept of "clinical economics" holds that significant economic benefit can come from small but narrowly targeted financial aid. Building economies from the bottom of the pyramid with financial aid targeted directly to small business entrepreneurs may prove to be a much more effective development strategy than giant top-down development projects. Imagine targeting $300 million in investment to one million small business entrepreneurs in a region in which most people live on $2 a day rather than to a giant national road construction project. One directly benefits the poor and trust that major economic development projects can grow from the ground up. The other directly benefits major economic development projects and trusts that benefits will trickle-down to the poor.

There are indications that the dominant macroeconomic paradigm is changing. Free trade and unguided economic growth are social forces that are powerful enough to address the world's most challenging economic problems. But they are forces that clearly have significant environmental and ethical costs. Sustainable development and sustainable economics seeks to channel the power of market economies to serve economic and ethical goals in ways that reduce environmental stress and harms. Within this new emerging framework, new models for business are beginning to develop. We turn now to some models for sustainable business.

ECOLOGICAL ECONOMICS AND CORPORATE SOCIAL RESPONSIBILITY

Economic theory has always developed in conjunction with social, political, and ethical worldviews. This is no less true for neoclassical economics than it is for ecological economics. Models for thinking about corporate social responsibility that depend on economic foundations will, accordingly, mirror those social, political, and ethical worldviews.

One can think of the conventional models of CSR in terms of expanding ethical constraints upon a general goal of increasing profits by responding to consumer demand. The alternative framework of sustainable corporate social responsibility replaces the goal of increasing profits with a goal of long-term sustainability. This echoes the position of Theodore Levitt quoted at the beginning of this chapter. Profits are a prerequisite for business, but are no more its purpose than breathing is the purpose of life. Business exists first and foremost as a means to supply human beings with what they need to live healthy and meaningful lives. A good business is one that accomplishes this goal efficiently and effectively over the long-term.

Reflect for a moment on conventional views of corporate social responsibility. At one extreme, we find the very narrow view associated with neoclassical economics. Business's social responsibility is to maximize profit by meeting consumer demand, and the only constraint is the duty to obey the law. At its most libertarian extreme, this view would also argue that the only appropriate laws are those that protect property and prohibit fraud and coercion. Theories of CSR become more moderate by expanding the range of constraints upon the pursuit of profit. Thus, one finds Norman Bowie, for example, arguing on Kantian grounds that beyond obedience to the law, business also has moral duties not to cause harm, even if not prohibited by law.[25] Various stakeholder theories essentially expand and develop this range of duties by identifying ethically legitimate stakeholders other than investors and by articulating the specific duties owed to them.

These theories can be accurately characterized as variations on the theme of balancing utilitarian ethics with an ethics of rights and duties. The pursuit of profit is the mechanism by which business is thought to serve the utilitarian goal of satisfying consumer demand and thereby maximizing the overall good. This utilitarian goal is itself to be constrained by the duties that one has to persons affected by these activities. Our duties to other people (and their rights) create side-constraints or boundaries on business activity; as long as business does not overstep those boundaries, it is free to pursue profit. Depending on the theory of rights and duties that one adopts, those constraints range from the minimal duty of obeying the law to more extensive accounts of duties associated with the stakeholder theory.

What one will not find among these common views is an account holding that business has positive duties either to *prevent* ecological harm or *to do* environmental good. Continuing the side-constraint and boundary metaphor, one does not find ethical goals determining either the direction or the substance of business activity. In essence, these views adopt an ethically passive model of business management in which managers can fulfill their responsibilities by actively doing little or nothing at all. Business passively *responds to* the demands of the market. Business is passive in *not violating the law*. Business is passive when it *causes no harm*. According to these views, the social responsibility of business requires business *to do* virtually nothing at all.

This point, of course, reminds us that both utilitarian and the ethics of rights and duties are thorough-going *liberal* theories of ethics. Philosophical liberalism denies that ethics can require anyone actually to do good; that would be asking too much of free and autonomous individuals. Ethics does not provide the goals of our behavior, only the limits. Liberty demands that we not coerce anyone to act in ways that they have not chosen, as long as their choices cause no harm to other individuals. Negative, not positive, duties are obligatory for every individual. Besides, given the wide variety of competing conceptions of the good life, there is little chance that we can arrive at a defensible and commonly accepted account of the good.

Thus, classic liberal theories tell us that doing good is supererogatory, an imperfect duty that we can encourage and praise but not require. Like charity, it is something that we hope for and encourage but not something that ethics obliges us to do. Unfortunately, many crucial environmental and ecological concerns are thought to fall within this sphere, particularly when the agent involved is business. Releasing toxic pollutants can be ethically prohibited, but preserving biological diversity, conserving natural resources, protecting wild and open spaces, reducing energy consumption, or designing fuel-efficient cars or sustainable production methods cannot. In fact, it is difficult to find many environmental concerns other than the ban on pollution that are thought to be part of business's social responsibility, and even that can be trumped when allowed by law. (CO_2 emissions being the obvious example—although they are known to cause harm, business is free to continue emitting copious amounts of this pollutant, because it is all quite legal.)

The alternative view holds that business does have an ethical responsibility, even when not required by law and not demanded by consumers, to redesign its operations in a way that is ecologically and economically sustainable over the long term. The ethical responsibilities of sustainable business provide the direction in which business develops as well as the constraints within which it operates. These positive ethical responsibilities are derived from the purpose and nature, or what traditional ethics would have called the *telos*, of business.

The narrow views of CSR sketched in earlier sections implicitly rely on a distinction between actively causing harm and passively allowing it to happen. As we have seen, most liberal theories hold individuals responsible for harms that they cause but not for harms that they allow to happen. Thus, although I may have a strong duty not to cause the starvation of my neighbor (a perfect duty in Kantian terms), I have no duty (an imperfect duty in Kantian terms) to prevent that starvation. Doing good is praiseworthy but not obligatory. But this distinction has been challenged, persuasively, by many philosophers.[26] Only the most ethically callous person would insist that we have no moral duty to prevent serious harm if in doing so we face only minor inconveniences.

I would like to suggest that something very much like this faces contemporary business institutions. Significant harm can be prevented, at present and into the near future, if business institutions would remake themselves on a model of sustainability. I would further claim that this is possible without putting most businesses in any greater financial jeopardy than is already and normally faced under the present model. Risks exist, of course, but there is no reason to think they are any graver than the risks normally faced every day by business entrepreneurs, managers, and business leaders.

Thus business managers have an ethical responsibility for taking positive actions to create a more just and environmentally sustainable world. This is a view consistent with ordinary understanding of business management and leadership. Business managers, of course, take an active leadership role all the time. Managers have a great deal of discretion in choosing both the ends of their business and the means by which those ends might be attained. If managerial prerogative means anything, it means that society expects and demands managerial professionals to exercise their judgment in determining the proper course for business. If the concepts of business leadership or entrepreneurship mean anything at all, they mean that business managers are widely understood to be capable of, and responsible for, taking positive actions. Which positive actions can we expect of ethically responsible managers? Theodore Levitt might have said those which create and keep customers. A sustainability answer suggests that business managers should pursue those actions that meet the needs of present customers without jeopardizing the ability of future customers to meet their own needs.

Endnotes

1 Theodore Levitt, "Marketing and the Public Purpose," *Vital Speeches of the Day*; 5/1/77, Vol. 43 Issue 14, p437, p. 7. I thank Lyla Hamilton of the University of Colorado for first calling my attention to this quote and helping me see its relevance to sustainability issues.

2 The International Society for Ecological Economics maintains a helpful website that includes an on-line encyclopedia of ecological economics. See http://www.ecoeco.org/publica/encyc.htm

3 *Ecological Economics: Concepts and Methods* Malte Faber, Reiner Manstellen, and John Proops (Edward Elgar Publishers, Cheltenham, UK. 1996), p. 10.

4 *An Introduction to Ecological Economics* by Robert Costanza, John Cumberland, Herman Daly, Robert Goodland, and Richard Norgaard (CRC Press, Boca Raton, FL, 1997), Ch. 3.

5 R.M. Solow, "An Almost Practical Step Towards Sustainability" A lecture delivered on the occasion of the fortieth anniversary of Resources for the Future, October 8, 1992, as quoted in Faber, *op. cit.*, p. 77.

6 K.E. Boulding "The Economics of the coming Spaceship Earth" in H. Jarrett (ed.), *Environmental Quality in a Growing Economy* pp. 3–14 (Baltimore, MD: Resources for the Future/Johns Hopkins University Press) 1966.

7   Herman Daly, *Beyond Growth* (Boston: Beacon Press, 1996), pp. 31–33.

8   Constanza et al., p. 80.

9   Ibid., p. 80.

10 Nicholas Georgescu-Roegen *The Entropy Law and the Economic Process* (Boston, Harvard University Press), 1971.

11 Hicks, J.R. *Value and Capital* (Oxford: Oxford University Press) p. 172.

12 For this discussion, I depend on Daly, *Beyond Growth*, chapter 4 and Costanza et al., *Ecological Economics*, chapter 3.

13 Daly, p. 77.

14 Information at http://www.rprogress.org/.

15 The ecological footprint quiz can be accessed at: http://www.myfootprint.org/.

16 See http://www.globalreporting.org/index.asp.

17 A very helpful review of many of the debates on globalization from a source generally sympathetic to it, can be found in "Globalization and its Critics," a special section of *The Economist*, September 29, 2001.

18 Jeffrey Sachs, *"The End of Poverty: Economic Possibilities for our Time,"* (Penguin Press, 2005).

19 Ibid., p. 26–27.

20 Sachs characterizes clinical economics as paying attention to the history, ethnography, and politics of individual countries and avoids imposing uniform policies regardless of the situation. Chapter 4.

21 At the time of the memo reprinted here, Lawrence Summers was the chief economist of the World Bank. In 1999, Mr. Summers was appointed Secretary of the Treasury by President Clinton. After the memo was leaked to the public, Mr. Summers apologized and explained that it was intended as ironic. Later reports even suggested that Mr. Summers had not even written the memo, although it was circulated with his name attached. In 2005, as president of Harvard University, Mr. Summers created a similar controversy when he expressed the view that women might not be as capable as men of doing scientific and mathematical research. In that case, Mr. Summer's defenders again claimed he was being ironic and expressing such views only as devil's advocate.

22 I owe these examples to Jacob Park, "Beyond Greening: Sustainability and the Information Revolution," an unpublished paper delivered at "Business and Environmental Sustainability" conference, University of Minnesota, Carlson School of Management, April 23, 2005. See also Ruediger Kuehr and Eric Williams, *Computers and the Environment* (Kluwer Academic Publishers, 2003). See, also, the video "Exporting Harm: The High-Tech Trashing of Asia" produced by the Basel Action Network, 2002 (http://www.ban.org/exportingharm_film.html).

23 These data are quoted from Muhammad Yunus, *Banker to the Poor: Micro-lending and the Battle against World Poverty*, (New York: Public Affairs Publishers, 1999), p. 145.

24 The following account is taken from *Banker to the Poor*, op. cit. The website for The Grameen Bank provides many other helpful resources to learn more about their projects and practices. http://www.grameen-info.org/bank/.

25 See Norman Bowie, "Morality, Money, and Motor Cars," cited previously.

26 The distinction rests upon the view that there is an ethically significant difference between acting and refraining, a distinction that has been seriously challenged. See, for example, the well-known essay by James Rachels, "Active and Passive Euthanasia" (*New England Journal of Medicine*, 1975) in which Rachels argues against the moral significance of this distinction as it has been employed in the ethics of euthanasia.

chapter six

The "Business Case" for Sustainability and Sustainable Business Models

INTRODUCTION

As we begin to consider how business might be restructured to meet its environmental responsibilities and become more sustainable, it is worth emphasizing a point made previously. We should not underestimate the range of managerial discretion. Business managers and executives enjoy a wide range of decision-making discretion. There are countless ways to pursue and attain profitability, even within a single firm or industry. We should abandon the assumption that environmental responsibilities are side-constraints on "the" pursuit of profit, as if there is only one way to pursue profits, and ethical responsibilities are a barrier to that. Rather, we should recognize that some avenues to profitability are environmentally risky, others environmentally prudent and sensible. Sustainable societies generate both new responsibilities and new opportunities for business in the twenty-first century.

As previously outlined, both history and ethics can encourage us to think of sustainability and business as a zero-sum game: environmentally sustainable decision comes at a cost of profitability; pursuing profits requires business managers to forgo environmental responsibility. Historically, most early environmental legislation followed this regulation-and-compliance model. Government passed laws that restrict business' freedom and business is forced to comply with such regulation. There is also a long tradition that assumes that ethical responsibilities conflict with self-interest. To be ethical, one must forgo self-interest; if one is pursuing self-interest, one is less than ethically praiseworthy. But the possibility exists that what is right in terms of sustainability may also be right in terms of business performance. One of the three pillars of sustainability, after all, is economic sustainability. If we expect business to address the significant global economic and environmental challenges of the twenty-first century, we need vibrant and stable (i.e., profitable) businesses. Simply put, a sustainable business must be a profitable business.

Fortunately, we have some good models for environmentally sustainable business practices. In this chapter, several models or frameworks for thinking about sustainable business are described. Some provide general guidelines for the goals of sustainable business, others offer more practical advice for the transition from the present economy into one guided by the principles of sustainable and ecological economics.

But before turning to several models for conceptualizing sustainable business, we need to address a values question only alluded to earlier. Is there a "business case" to be made for sustainable business? Providing new models for reconceptualizing business presumes that there are good reasons for making such changes. Chapter Two provided both the factual and ethical rationale for thinking that a more sustainable business and economic model is needed. Within that context, I made the claim that there can be good self-interested reasons for valuing the environment. This chapter offers a more direct version of that claim. There are good business reasons for the evolution of business toward sustainability.

The Business Case for Sustainability

The sustainability paradigm starts with the assumption that the time is approaching when business institutions will either evolve into more sustainable enterprises or will simply cease to exist. The two forces of increasing social demand for goods and services and the decreasing ability of the biosphere to provide resources to meet that demand are approaching a point at which they will merge. That assumption is less a prediction of doom than it is an observation of present realities. But forward-looking, creative, and entrepreneurial companies will recognize this trend as offering tremendous opportunities rather than as creating barriers.

Barring a catastrophe, society will survive and vibrant businesses must play a role in that survival. All models for sustainable development envision a central role for business in a sustainable future. It will, after all, be the businesses of the next industrial revolution that meet the real needs of the billions of people living in that sustainable future. The businesses that survive in this sustainable world will be businesses that anticipate this change and adapt to it on their own terms.

The models discussed in what follows share common themes that give some indication where these changes will occur. Business products and operations should be modeled on biological processes. "Closed-loop" manufacturing, biomimicry, elimination of wastes, and discovering ways to treat wastes as a resource are different aspects of sustainable business. One implication of these proposals is that new business opportunities exist for realizing new business synergies when the wastes of one firm become the resources of others. Another implication is that great cost savings can be found by looking to reduce and eliminate wastes.

Another theme shared by sustainable business models will involve the reduction in flows through the production process. Improved efficiencies, dematerialization, reduction of energy use, and a shift to sustainable energy products will improve industry's health, much in the way that improved blood circulation improves a person's health. These shared themes, of course, have economic as well as ecological and ethical implications.

Some critics would see the attempt to make a business case for sustainability as a surrender to corporate interests or as a sign that sustainability has been co-opted by business. If the business case involves an attempt to convince any and every business that it can flourish within a sustainable economy, that might be true. But not every contemporary business, product, or industry will or should survive into a sustainable future. The question of sustainable business is as much about what business will become in the future as it is about how each and every business can become sustainable.

Some philosophers might also be skeptical about a business case for sustainability. Self-interest, according to some, conflicts with moral considerations, and if one acts out of self-interest one is, by that fact, not acting morally. But with a more robust understanding of the "self" of self-interest, one that has more in common with Platonic ethics than Kantian moral philosophy, this conflict is more apparent than real. Were business to fulfill its true purpose in a sustainable economy, doing the right thing coincides ethically with doing what is in a business's self-interest. Sustainable practices conflict with business's self-interest only if the business "self" is a short-term and constricted understanding of the nature of business. If the purpose of business is understood in sustainable terms, it will turn out that sustainable practices are in a firm's self-interests.

With that said, some persuasive reasons can be offered to the business community for why it should move in the direction of sustainability. First, of course, is the huge market represented by the billions of human beings who face unmet needs on a daily basis. All too often, economists and business managers conceptualize consumer demand in ways that ignore the needs of the billions of human beings who lack food, clothing, shelter, medical care, jobs. There are enormous opportunities waiting for the businesses who respond to this market.

A convincing and detailed case for how this might happen has been made by business scholar C.K. Prahalad in his book, *"The Fortune at the Bottom of the Pyramid."*[1] Prahalad and others have argued that entrepreneurial and creative businesses are finding ways to develop markets among the world's poorest people. The 4 billion people comprising the base of the pyramid (the phrase changed by Stuart Hart to avoid the pejorative-sounding "bottom"[2]) provide a market so large and diverse that it can only be addressed in ways that are environmentally sustainable. It will simply be impossible to meet those needs with products and services that are resource and energy intensive, environmentally destructive, or socially insensitive. Sustainable enterprises will find huge markets at the base of the pyramid that unsustainable business and industry will be unable to satisfy.

Stuart Hart offers as an example the potential automotive market in emerging economies such as China and India.[3] Automotive corporations could approach these markets with their present business models and seek to sell large gasoline-powered automobiles. To do this, the automotive firms would need to restrict their marketing to the very top of the economic pyramid in emerging economies for two reasons. First, only the economically affluent would be able to afford such luxuries and, second, such densely populated regions and emerging economies simply could never support the widespread reliance on internal-combustion engines. Emerging economies lack the energy and transportation infrastructure to support widespread use of automobiles, and the environmental consequences of doing so would be disastrous.

But consider what might happen if the automotive industry approached these markets in terms of the billions of potential customers at the base of the economic pyramid. This market would require vehicles that are inexpensive and reliant on clean-energy sources. Given the sheer populations size of the base of the pyramid, even these initiatives might fail as a result of congestion and gridlock. To take advantage of the transportation market emerging in such countries as China or India, the automotive industry will need to develop even more creative and sustainable products and strategies. As Hart suggests:

> "Because China's energy and transportation infrastructures are still being defined, there is an opportunity to leapfrog to clean technology, yielding important environmental, public health, and competitive benefits. . . . Sustainability will require new transportation solutions for the needs of emerging economies with huge populations. This might feature entirely new products and services designed to make smaller cities and villages more economically viable so that mass migration to megacities becomes unnecessary and even undesirable. Will the giants of the auto industry be prepared for such radical change, or will they leave the field to new ventures that are not encumbered by the competencies of the past?"[4]

Beyond the unlimited opportunity for new markets, there are many potential cost savings available from the move toward sustainability. Significant savings can follow from eliminating wastes, reducing operating expenses, and striving toward eco-efficiency. Waste is a bad thing, both ecologically and financially. A company that reduces and eliminates its wastes will reduce its costs. A company that finds ways to turn waste into a new resource will increase its revenues from already existing assets.

The practical side of cost savings can be seen in the well-known example of Interface. Interface Corporation's movement toward sustainability initiated by CEO Ray Anderson in the early 1990s did result in increased efficiencies and reduced costs. In the late 1990s however, Interface entered into a 3-year period of decreasing sales and lost revenues. Interface's primary market sells carpeting to office and commercial buildings. During the economic recession of these years, office and commercial expansion declined, and Interface's business suffered as a result. However, Interface credits the increased efficiencies and reduced costs of their sustainability initiatives with a major role in helping the business to weather the economic downturn. Every business experiences challenging economic periods and, as this Interface example demonstrates, cost savings associated with the move toward sustainability can provide a cushion against the normal downturns of the business cycle.

Sustainability also creates opportunities to decrease capital costs in building or remodeling facilities. Buildings designed from the start to be energy efficient, with bright, airy, and well-ventilated space will decrease costs and improve efficiencies over the long term. William McDonough and Michael Braungart's work with a new manufacturing plant for Herman Miller, a large office furniture maker, is a case in point. Herman Miller has a long tradition of socially responsible practices and has worked with McDonough and Braungart's cradle-to-cradle design protocol to develop truly sustainable furniture products. But in the early 1990s, Herman Miller also worked with McDonough to design and build their new manufacturing plant in Michigan. The new design has paid dividends in the form of lower energy costs and increased worker productivity. Herman Miller has also been instrumental in creating the United States Green Building Council (USGBC) in 1993. The Council describes itself as "the nation's foremost coalition of leaders from across the building industry working to promote buildings that are environmentally responsible, profitable and healthy places to live and work."[5]

Sustainable companies can also acquire competitive advantages. Not only would increased savings, revenues, and efficiencies place a company in a better position relative to its competitors, but sustainable companies are poised to take advantage of "green" and sustainable markets. Sustainable practices should not be only a marketing tool, of course, but one should not underestimate the growing consumer market for sustainable and environmentally beneficial products and services.

Another aspect of the competitive advantages of sustainability lies in the labor market. Herman Miller discovered that their green building became very popular with employees. Improved morale, increased employee loyalty, and, simply, healthier and more attractive working conditions for employees were added benefits of McDonough's sustainable design principles.

Business should also recognize the real possibility of future government regulation that may well require steps toward sustainability. The companies already involved in sustainable practices are likely to play leadership roles in fashioning future standards. Again, Herman Miller provides an excellent example. In 1993, Herman Miller was a founding sponsor of the United States Green Building Council (USGBC). The USGBC is a nonprofit organization of architects, construction companies, engineering firms, and others in the building industry committed to promoting "environmentally responsible, and healthy buildings for business and homes." The USGBC developed the LEED rating system (Leadership in Energy and Environmental Design), a voluntary classification system of common standards for creating and measuring sustainable buildings. The USGBC used Herman Miller's manufacturing plant designed by Bill McDonough as a model for the LEED certification and rating process. Today, there is a growing movement, especially among state and local governments, to require new construction to conform to minimal LEED standards.

In the past, many companies waited until environmental regulations coerced them into action. At that point, many were overwhelmed by the costs of clean-up and compensation. Companies that wait take similar risks and will likely deal with sustainability as a compliance issue. By taking the initiative in designing and constructing a sustainable building, Herman Miller helped create and set the standards that less innovative companies will not be challenged to meet.

Finally, avoiding future legal liability provides another business reason for the move toward sustainability. There is no better means for managing both regulatory and legal risks than by being proactive in taking steps to prevent problems from occurring. The legal concepts of negligence and forseeability are just waiting to be exploited in holding business liable for the entire life cycle of its products. As municipalities struggle to find ways to dispose of solid wastes, an obvious strategy will be to turn to the businesses who designed, manufactured, and sold those products and hold them accountable to take-back their products, or pay for their proper disposal.

Legal developments in Europe and elsewhere already foreshadow this future. Beginning in the early 1990s, several countries have passed legislation mandating producer responsibility for the wastes created by their products. Variously referred to as "take-back" laws or "extended producer responsibility," such laws require that business be responsible financially, if not physically, for the eventual disposal or recycling of products that they place into the market.

Spurred on by the European Union's Waste Electrical and Electronic Equipment (WEEE) and Restriction of Hazardous Substances (RoHS) directives, more than 20 European countries have already passed laws that encourage or require manufacturers to take responsibility for the eventual disposal of such products as batteries, electronics, fluorescent lights, appliances such as refrigerators and air conditioners, televisions, and automobiles. Japan, South Korea, and Taiwan have similar legislation.

Business executives who do not anticipate such developments on a wider scale by beginning to redesign their products in ways that make reuse and recycling easier and even profitable are not acting as very prudent risk managers.

MODELS FOR SUSTAINABLE BUSINESS: NATURAL CAPITALISM AND INDUSTRIAL ECOLOGY

In recent years, the more practical side of sustainable business has been described in many forums and in many books. The sustainable circular flow model described on page 57, as well as the insights of ecological economics, provide useful guidelines for conceptualizing sustainable business practices. Several of these approaches worth considering are natural capitalism, industrial ecology, the Natural Step, and cradle-to-cradle design.

In *Natural Capitalism*, authors Paul Hawken, Amory Lovins, and Hunter Lovins provide a conceptual model for, and numerous examples of, sustainable business practices.[6] *Natural Capitalism* offers four guiding principles for the redesign of business. First, the productivity of natural resources must and can be dramatically increased. This constitutes a further development of what is sometimes called "eco-efficiency." A second principle, called "biomimicry" or "closed-loop design," requires that business be redesigned to model biological processes. Byproducts formerly lost as waste and pollution must be eliminated, reintegrated into the production process, or returned as a benign or beneficial product to the biosphere. Third, traditional models of business as producers of goods should be replaced with a model of business as a provider of services. The old economy focuses on producing goods (e.g., light bulbs and carpets) when consumer demand really focuses on services (e.g., illumination and floor-covering). This shift can provide significant incentives for accomplishing the first two goals. Additionally, business must reinvest in natural capital. As any introductory textbook in business management teaches, responsible managers and executives reinvest in productive capital. Because traditional economic models have ignored the origin of natural capital, they have neglected to include reinvestment in natural capital as part of prudent business practice. An environmentally responsible business must address this shortcoming.

Both eco-efficiency and biomimicry can be understood in terms of Figure B, printed on page 57. Eco-efficient management would discover ways to reduce the rate at which natural resources flow through the economic system. *Natural Capitalism* contains numerous examples in which managerial decisions regarding the design of both products and production methods has increased resource efficiency by a factor of 5, 10, and in some cases even 100. The standard growth model of economic development tells us that we could meet the needs of the poorest 75 percent of the world's population by increasing economic growth by a factor of 5 to 10. Eco-efficent business practice aims for the same end by increasing efficiency, and therefore decreasing resource use, by a factor of 5 to 10.

Examples of eco-efficiency can be found in many areas of business operations. Business managers must find ways to meet consumer demand with fewer resources. A simple example would be a housing developer who designs a neighborhood with cluster housing, green spaces, habitat corridors, and biking trails instead of the traditional "cookie-cutter" development pattern. Each development pattern can be profitable but one is more environmentally destructive than the other. Energy demand is another particularly apt example for this responsibility. *Natural Capitalism* describes the redesign of an industrial pumping system at Interface Corporation. With an eye toward reducing energy demand, the redesign with larger and straighter pipes resulted in a 92 percent, or 12-fold, energy savings. Energy-efficient windows, lighting, motors, and insulation in the design and upgrade of every building would greatly reduce overall energy use while still meeting present production targets.

Ecoefficiency alone is only part of the solution. At best, eco-efficiency can help a firm reduce wastes. The principle of biomimicry attempts to eliminate the wastes produced by even eco-efficient production processes. As occurs in biological systems, biomimicry in business would turn the wastes of one activity into a useful resource for another. Business managers have a responsibility to seek ways to integrate former wastes back into the production system, transform wastes into biologically beneficial elements, or, minimally, to produce wastes at rates no faster than the biosphere can absorb them. An interesting example involves wastes from a chicken processing plant.

Gold'n Plump Poultry is one of the largest poultry producers in the Midwest. The Gold'n Plump plant in Cold Spring, Minnesota, processes 4 million pounds of chicken each week, primarily for the retail grocery store market. Chicken processing is a water-intensive industry, and the Gold'n Plump plant is located along the banks of the Sauk River. A wastewater treatment facility is located at the plant where water is cleaned before being discharged back into the river. As in all water treatment plants, large amounts of solid wastes are produced in the process. Traditionally, such solids were sold to local farmers to be spread as fertilizer on croplands, a practice that was preferable to disposal in landfills, but which also had some environmental downside. Run-off and seepage into groundwater were potential pollution problems, and unpleasant odors and high transportation costs made the process less than ideal.

Two local entrepreneurs recognized a business opportunity in the solid wastes produced by Gold'n Plump. This waste material could provide the resources for the products of another company. Material that was initially a problem for Gold'n Plump to dispose became a product to be sold. Mississippi Topsoils located their high-tech composting business adjacent to the Gold'n Plump plant. Gold'n Plump sends over 100,000 pounds of solid wastes each week to Mississippi Topsoils, where it is combined with residential yard waste, sawdust, and clean scrap wood collected from public and private recycling efforts in giant state-of-the-art composting containers to create compost. Most of the additional material, often freely given to the company, would otherwise have ended up in landfills or incinerators. Mississippi Topsoils turns what would have been wasted into high-quality compost, which is sold to wholesale nurseries and landscapers, farmers, and home garden centers. Mississippi Topsoils and Gold'n Plump uncovered a good business opportunity by mimicking a fundamental fact of biological nature: in nature, nothing is wasted because wastes of one process become nutrients for another.[7]

In many ways, challenges of eco-efficiency and biomimicry are challenges of business design. A well-publicized test case of such sustainable design principles is taking place at Ford Motor Company's Rouge River industrial complex. This $2 billion redesign, overseen by environmental architect and designer William McDonough, will introduce sustainable principles to one of the world's largest industrial complexes. Reinvestment in productive capital is a basic economic responsibility for every business manager. Doing so in the way that Ford intends, in a way that addresses environmental and social concerns as well as economic ones, should be among the ethical responsibilities of every business manager.

The third principle of sustainable business practice may require a greater paradigm shift in business management. Traditional manufacturing aims to produce goods; this new model shifts to providing services. This shift, according to *Natural Capitalism*, will reinforce principles of both eco-efficiency and biomimicry. Traditional economic and managerial models interpret consumer demand as the demand for products—for example, washing machines, carpets, lights, consumer electronics, air conditioners, cars, computers, and so forth. A service-based economy interprets consumer demand as a demand for services—for example, for clothes cleaning, floor-covering, illumination, entertainment, cool air, transportation, word processing, and so forth. *Natural Capitalism* provides examples of businesses that have made such a shift in each of these industries. This change produces incentives for product redesigns that create more durable and more easily recyclable products.

One of the best examples of this shift can also be seen at Interface. Interface is making a transition from selling carpeting to leasing floor-covering services. On a traditional business model, carpet is sold to consumers who, once they become dissatisfied with the color or style, or once the carpeting becomes worn, dispose of the carpet. Ultimately, the carpet would end up in landfills. There is little incentive on this model to produce long-lasting or easily recyclable carpeting. In fact, the "planned obsolescence" approach would seem to make more sense by encouraging a quicker turnover of customer demand. Once Interface shifted to leasing floor-covering services, incentives were created to produce long-lasting, easily replaceable and recyclable carpets. If Interface is contractually required by their lease to replace worn-out carpeting, they have a strong incentive to create more durable products. If they are obligated to replace the carpeting, modular carpet tiles are a more efficient product than wide broadlooms. If they take the carpet back, having safe and recyclable products protects their employees and provides the business with new and almost cost-free resource. Interface thereby accepts responsibility for the entire life cycle of the product it markets. Because they retain ownership and are responsible for maintenance, Interface strives to produce carpeting that can be easily replaced in sections rather than in its entirety, that is more durable, and that can eventually be remanufactured. Redesigning their carpets and shifting to a service lease has also improved production efficiencies and reduced material and energy costs significantly. Consumers benefit by getting what they truly desire at lower costs and fewer burdens.

The final element of the natural capitalism model advises business to invest in natural capital. As described in the previous chapter, traditional economics distinguished between fixed, working, and financial capital. These capital items are considered those factors that, along with labor and resources, produce a stream of goods, services, and income. The advice to invest in natural capital stems from the recognition that we are approaching a historical point at which natural resources rather than labor, finances, or technology becomes the limiting factor in economic productivity.[8] Prudent business managers make investments in those areas that most limit productive capacity. Thus, at times when labor is cheap, prudent managers might build new factories. When skilled labor is scarce, prudent managers invest in training programs for employees. As the world approaches the biophysical limits of economic growth, prudent business managers will look for ways to invest in the productive capacity of nature. This strategy might include seeking substitutes for nonrenewable resources and a greater reliance on renewables, especially in the energy sector. It might also seek ways to integrate biological processes in buildings, operations, and production.

Another approach to sustainable business that builds on many similar principles has come to be called industrial ecology.[9] Industrial ecology is a movement among industrial engineers that aims to integrate ecological models into industrial design and production. An early description of the field, defined an industrial ecosystem as one in which "the use of energies and materials is optimized, wastes and pollution are minimized, and there is an economically viable role for every product of a manufacturing process."[10] A common theme in this field is the rejection of linear manufacturing models in which resources are extracted, processed into products, and eventually disposed back into the ecosystem. This "take-make-waste" model is replaced with circular or cyclical patterns of industrial production.

A major part of this movement seeks to integrate various industries in ways that the byproducts and wastes of one become the productive resources of another. The relationship between Gold'n Plump Poultry and Mississippi Topsoils described previously, would be a perfect example of such symbiotic merging of businesses. Many local communities are moving toward the creation of "ecological industrial parks," an attempt to transform the traditional concept of an industrial park. "Eco-industrial parks" aim to attract businesses that can work together in a symbiotic relationship similar to Gold 'n Plump and Mississippi Topsoils.

In practice, industrial ecology develops specific technical tools to help managers and engineers measure, assess, design, and implement strategies of sustainable manufacturing. As described in an influential essay on industrial ecology, these processes

> "involve 'closing loops' by recycling, making maximum use of recycled materials in new production, optimizing use of materials and embedded energy, minimizing waste generation, and reevaluating "wastes" as raw material for other processes. They also imply more than simple "one-dimensional" recycling of a single material or product—as with, for example, aluminum beverage can recycling. In effect, they represent "multidimensional" recycling, or the creation of complex "food webs" between companies and industries."[11]

MODELS FOR SUSTAINABLE BUSINESS: THE NATURAL STEP AND CRADLE-TO-CRADLE

Another approach to sustainable business practices has been developed as "The Natural Step" by Swedish physician Karl-Henrik Robert.[12] Robert began developing this approach in the 1980s while working as a medical doctor conducting cancer research. He was motivated by two seemingly paradoxical realities. First, he was struck by the passionate concern he witnessed of parents and families for their children suffering from cancer. But, the wider community seemed to pay little attention or concern to protecting and preserving the natural environment for the sake of our children's future. Second, he could see why business could be blamed for much environmental destruction, but knew that restoring the environment would be unlikely without the contributions from the economic engine of contemporary business.

The Natural Step organization works with businesses to develop strategies for the transformation to sustainability. They begin with four fundamental principles, or "systems conditions," to provide a framework for understanding sustainable practices. Working with companies, they encourage businesses to create a vision of what that firm would be like if it were sustainable, and then "back-casts" (as opposed to "forecasts") how to get to that vision from the present state.

The four system conditions are versions of familiar principles. "In order for society to be sustainable, nature's functions and diversity are not systematically:

1. Subject to increasing concentrations of substances extracted from the Earth's crust;
2. Subject to increasing concentrations of substances produced by society; or
3. Impoverished by over-harvesting or other forms of ecosystem manipulation;
4. And resources are used fairly and efficiently in order to meet basic human needs worldwide."[13]

The first two principles address the rates at which natural resources are extracted from the Earth and human-created wastes deposited back into the biosphere. The third principle addresses the preservation of the earth's productivity, and the fourth acknowledges the connections between ecological sustainability and social equity.

The Natural Step framework asks us to visualize the present environmental and economic situation in terms of a giant funnel created by two converging sloping lines.[14] The top line represents the availability of resources and is sloping downward along an x axis from left to right. The bottom line represents societal demand for those resources, and is represented by an upward-sloping line along the same axis. As overall social demand increases, the availability of resources to meet that demand decreases. Sustainability could be represented when the slope of these lines turns parallel along the horizontal. As the two sloping lines converge, the available options for business decrease. A forward-looking business decides what is needed to become sustainable at an early stage when the room to maneuver within the converging lines remains wide.

In many ways, the Natural Step framework is forward-looking and hopeful. The suggestion is that business today still has room to maneuver between the increasing social demands for resources and the decreasing capacity of ecosystems to provide those resources. But these two trends are approaching the point at which the gap narrows and the opportunities will shrink. Barring a catastrophe, there will come a time when businesses must, voluntarily or otherwise, be transformed into sustainable enterprises. The proactive, entrepreneurial, and creative business must begin to envision how they will operate in the age of sustainability. Given that vision, such innovative companies today begin the process of transformation. Business is already familiar with financial and market forecasts, a process in which present trends are extrapolated into the future in the attempt to predict what will happen. The Natural Step's "back-cast" begins with the future visions, and then works out the trends and steps needed to arrive at that destination. Given differing companies, industries, and social contexts, the Natural Step encourages individual firms to work out the specifics of their own individual transformation.

Another practical framework for thinking about the transformation to sustainable business is associated with the work of architect and designer William McDonough and chemist Michael Braungart.[15] McDonough and Braungart have worked with many companies to help design truly sustainable, cradle-to-cradle firms. Among their clients are Nike, Ford Motor Company, Oberlin College, British Petroleum, BASF, Herman Miller, Designtex, Rohner Textil, Pendleton, and Milliken & Co.

In their writings, McDonough and Braungart frame both the ecological failures of the old industrial revolution and the future challenges of sustainability as design questions. Wastes, pollution, inefficiencies, environmental destruction, toxic by-products are all failures in the design of products and production processes. A well-designed product or a well-designed industry has no waste. The "next industrial revolution" will eliminate rather than reduce wastes and rely on renewable and non-pollution sources of energy. In a phrase that is closely associated with their work, "waste equals food."

The McDonough and Braungart approach encourages business to think of each product as having a life-cycle: they are envisioned, designed, created, brought to the market, used, and eventually disposed of as their useful life comes to an end. Life-cycle analysis examines each step along this cycle, looking for opportunities to improve the sustainability—economic, ecological, and ethical—of the product. Typically, the life-cycle of each product is understood in terms of "cradle-to-grave." The product is brought to life, used, and then dies. McDonough and Braungart argue that we should replace the cradle-to-grave metaphor with a cradle-to-cradle metaphor in which the product is designed in such a way that at the end of its useful life what remains becomes the resources for a new product. Just as the natural biological cycle uses topsoil created from decaying plants to provide nourishment for new plant growth, cradle-to-cradle design looks for ways to turn industrial wastes into new resources.

The emphasis on mimicking biological processes is a consistent theme with all these approaches. But McDonough and Braungart have reservations about other aspects of some environmental and sustainable practices. The common environmental guidance to "reduce, reuse, recycle" and to "do more with less" address the problems with current practices without getting at the bad designs that underlie and cause the problems. If what we reuse, recycle, or use less of is ecologically detrimental, then we are still participating in an unsustainable practice. Ecoefficiency is not a solution if the production process made more efficient is itself harmful or noxious. Growth is only a problem if what is grown is harmful; tree growth is ecologically beneficial; cancer growth is not.

McDonough and Braungart's work is also hopeful about the future and particularly about the business and economic opportunities offered by the sustainability revolution. Properly designed sustainable products will either be composed of materials that are nontoxic and degradable into biological nutrients, or of synthetic materials that are safely and completely recycled back into industry as "technical nutrients." When the end product is fully returned into biological or technical systems, when waste equals food in other words, business can continue indefinitely. This style of economic growth is sustainable according to McDonough and Braungart. Rather than criticize business for past practices, McDonough and Braungart rely on business to help bring about the sustainable future.

The individuals, the businesses, and the organizations mentioned in this chapter demonstrate that the movement towards sustainable business has already begun. This movement will create many new opportunities for creative and entrepreneurial business. But, like the first industrial revolution, it will also create unforeseen managerial challenges and responsibilities. In the following chapters, we'll consider where business management and business ethics might be headed in this new era.

Endnotes

1 *"The Fortune at the Bottom of the Pyramid: Eradicating Poverty through Profits,"* by C.K. Prahalad (Upper Saddle River, NJ: Wharton School Publishing, 2005). See also Prahalad and Stuart Hart, "The Fortune at the Bottom of the Pyramid" *Strategy and Business* 26 (2002): 54–67; and Prahalad and Allen Hammond, "Serve the World's Poor, Profitably," *Harvard Business Review* (September, 2002).

2 Stuart Hart, *"Capitalism at the Crossroads"* (Upper Saddle River, NJ: Wharton School Publishing, 2005), p. 108, footnote 4.

3 Ibid., pp. 77–78.

4 Ibid., p. 78.

5 Information about Herman Miller's long tradition of working towards sustainability can be found on the company's website: http://www.hermanmiller.com/. The United States Green Building Council also maintains a helpful website, with links to local affiliates, at: http://www.usgbc.org/.

6 *Natural Capitalism*, Paul Hawken, Amory Lovins, Hunter Lovins (New York: Little Brown) 1999.

7 Information on Mississippi Topsoils come from interviews the owner, Brad Matuska. Other information can be found at http://www.mississippitopsoils .com/. For more on biomimicry, see *Biomimicry: Innovation Inspired by Nature*, by Janine M. Benyus (New York: William Morrow and Co., Inc., 1997).

8 An economic explanation of this claim can be found in Daly, *Beyond Growth*, chapter 4.

9 Two classic essays in this field are: "Industrial Ecology: An Environmental Agenda for Industry," by Hardin Tibbs (Arthur D. Little, Inc. 1991). "Strategies For Manufacturing," by Robert A. Frosch, and Nicholas E. Gallopoulos. *Scientific American* 189(3):152, 1989. See also the International Society for Industrial Ecology, http://www.is4ie.org//.

10 Frosch and Gallopoulos, p. 152.

11 Tibbs, "Industrial Ecology, " p. 10.

12 Two helpful resources for understanding the Natural Step and for case studies of businesses employing Natural Step strategies are: *The Natural Step for Business: Wealth, Ecology, and the Evolutionary Corporation*, by Brian Nattrass and Mary Altomare (British Columbia: New Society Publishers, 1999), and *Ants, Galileo, and Gandhi: Designing the Future of Business Through Nature Genius, and Compassion* edited by Sissel Waage (Sheffield, U.K., Greenleaf Publishing 2003). Robert's work is summarized in his *The Natural Step Story: Seeding a Quiet Revolution* (British Columbia: New Society Press, 2002). Updated information can be found at: http://www.naturalstep.org/

13 *The Natural Step for Business*, p. 23.

14 See, for example, *The Natural Step for Business*, pp. 18–19.

15 *Cradle to Cradle: Remaking the Way We Make Things*, by William McDonough and Michael Braungart (North Point Press, April 2002) and "The Next Industrial Revolution" by William McDonough and Michael Braungart, *The Atlantic Monthly* October 1998.

chapter seven

Sustainable Production and Sustainable Products

INTRODUCTION

In the first six chapters, the more theoretical case for reconceptualizing business in a way that is compatible with ecological economics was presented. In the following chapters, we look at more practical and managerial issues in creating a sustainable business. We also consider a range of ethical issues that arise in this context. We begin with an examination of the responsibilities that business has for unsustainable products and production methods.

Conventional economic wisdom places much of the responsibility for products with the consumers who demand them. Supply, we are told, is a function of demand. Thus, from this perspective, the appearance of sustainable products will have to wait for consumer demand or government mandates. But there are good reasons for rejecting this view.

First, it is a mistake to treat business as a passive spectator responding to, rather than creating and shaping, consumer demand. Consumers can demand only that which they know about and, to a large extent, only that which is available in the marketplace. Business clearly plays an active role in creating each of these conditions. Through marketing, business informs consumers and influences consumer demand. Furthermore, consumer demand is most often generic; consumers want a car, or, even more generally, transportation, not necessarily a Ford or an internal combustion engine. Consumers desire headache relief, not necessarily acetaminophen or Tylenol. Consumers demand convenient food, not necessary a fast-food restaurant in a strip mall. Business, therefore, has options for determining how to satisfy consumer demand and has the ability to help shape that demand.

We already know that there is a huge under-served market for sustainable goods and services. Billions of people at the base of the global economic pyramid have tremendous unmet needs that creative products and marketing have not yet addressed. This is a case in which there is great demand, but few suppliers yet responding.

Next, even if we accept the conventional view that consumers bear primary responsibility for sustainable products, business would not be able to escape some ethical responsibility for such products. Independent of products themselves is the process by which those goods and services are produced. Businesses have wide discretion regarding how their products get produced. The production process itself creates a challenge, opportunity, and responsibility for creating a sustainable business. Even when consumers demand a specific product, how that product is manufactured, the working conditions of the people who make it, the resources that go into production, the wastes that are left behind, how the product is designed, and how the product is commercialized, transported, and retailed are all areas in which business can move toward sustainability.

Additionally, businesses themselves are consumers, relying on other businesses in their supply chain for a wide range of products for their operations. Every business is a consumer and must take responsibility for demanding sustainable products from its suppliers. Business cannot disavow responsibility for sustainable products by allocating that duty to consumers without taking on the same responsibility for itself when it acts as a consumer in purchasing products from other businesses. In recent years, business has been held accountable for supply chain activities concerning sweatshop working conditions and genetically modified organisms. We have every reason to think that a similar approach will be taken concerning supply-chain responsibility for sustainable products.

SUSTAINABLE PRODUCTS

Perhaps the major criterion by which one can judge a product as sustainable lies with the production and marketing process itself. A product is sustainable if it is designed, produced, and marketed in ways that do not decrease the ability of people to meet their own needs in the future. Thus, agricultural products that do not degrade the ecosystems on which they rely would be sustainable. Buildings designed to meet Leadership in Energy and Environmental Design (LEED) standards for sustainable design would be sustainable. Import products that meet fair-trade standards would be sustainable. We consider these production and marketing issues in more detail in the following sections.

But are there other ways to assess products themselves as sustainable? In general, we could say that sustainable products are those goods and services that meet the real needs of human beings without decreasing the capacity of the biosphere to continue producing the goods and services needed by others. Beyond this fairly general definition, we might think in terms of assessing the sustainability of products in terms of both the material of the product and its purpose or use. What is the product made from, and how is it used?

Products made from materials that can be toxic to humans and other living things are, over the long term, unsustainable. For example, studies have shown widespread contamination of human breast milk with residues of such toxic elements as polychlorinated biphenyls (PCBs), DDT, dioxins, dibenzofurans, polybrominated diphenyl ethers (PBDEs), and heavy metals.[1] Each of these types of compounds have serious health consequences for human beings. Products containing such chemicals, and the chemicals themselves, must be phased out as we move toward a sustainable economy. Products made from natural, renewable, and biodegradable material are sustainable in ways that synthetic compounds derived from nonrenewable and nonbiodegradable sources are not. Thus, cotton, wool, hemp, and silk (when produced in a sustainable manner and not treated with toxic flame retardants and dyes) are sustainable in ways that synthetic plastics are not.

As mentioned in the previous chapter, William McDonough and Michael Braungart have developed a design protocol that can be used to assess the sustainability of products and materials.[2] McDonough and Braungart suggest a variety of criteria that measure the health and environmental impact of the materials used in products. Materials that are carcinogenic are unsustainable, as are materials that harm the ozone layer, contribute to the greenhouse effect, or that bioaccumulate in food chains.

Beyond a product's materials, we can also judge sustainability in terms of a products purpose or use. Some products directly contribute to the creation of a sustainable economy; others hinder that movement. Renewable energy sources such as fuel cell, solar-power, and wind-power generators are products that would be part of a sustainable future. Nutritious food would be sustainable in ways that high-fat, non-nutritious junk food is not.

Of course, many products are mere instruments that can be used in numerous ways, some of which are sustainable, others less so. Computers, information technology, and electronics can be used in countless ways to create a more sustainable future, and they can be used in ways that lead to social and environmental degradation. Genetically modified crops and seeds can be used to support sustainable agriculture, or they can be used to monopolize agricultural power. The internal combustion, fossil fuel–dependent engine can be used in farm machinery to support poor farmers, but ultimately such technology cannot be sustained without creating serious environmental harm.

As we turn now to some of the ethical aspects of sustainable production, it will be helpful to remember the framework for sustainable business introduced in Chapter Six. In general, the production process should mimic biological processes in which resources are not used, nor wastes generated at rates beyond what the biosphere can produce or absorb them. Increased efficiencies are also crucial not only to contribute to the financial bottom line but to help reduce resource use and waste. Investing in natural capital, treating the productivity and diversity of the natural world as capital rather than income, will also reap long-term economic and ecological benefits.

SUSTAINABLE PRODUCTION: POLLUTION AND WASTE

One of the implications of the diagram on page 57 as well as the observations concerning entropy offered by ecological economics is that every business activity will inevitably have waste by-products. At a minimum, the amount of useful energy that goes into the production process is inexorably and relentlessly degraded. All production processes involve by-products—wastes and pollution—that remain. The challenge for sustainable business is to find ways to minimize, eliminate, or reuse as much of these by-products as possible.

A helpful place to begin thinking about the ethical aspects of pollution and wastes is the landmark environmental case involving Reserve Mining Company. Reserve Mining, located along the northern shore of Lake Superior in Silver Bay, Minnesota, processed low-grade iron ore called taconite into a form suitable for steel production. Processing taconite involves crushing large quantities of taconite rock into a fine-grain dust, mixing that dust with large quantities of water taken from Lake Superior, and flushing this through a series of magnets and filters that separate out most of the iron particles. The iron is then processed into tiny pellets that are shipped off to steel mills. The remaining rock and dust, referred to as "tailings," was originally discharged back into Lake Superior as wastewater. More than two tons these tailings were generated for every ton of iron retrieved.

When the company began operation in the late 1940s, its production process was uncontroversial. There was no evidence that the tailings discharged into Lake Superior were harmful in any way, and the lake itself seemed big enough and deep enough to absorb them. Silver Bay is located just ashore of some of the deepest underwater trenches in all of Lake Superior. The wastes themselves seemed harmless because they contained nothing other than water and the used portion of the natural rock and minerals taken from the land adjacent to Lake Superior. Reserve Mining obtained the necessary permits and operated without problems for more than 20 years, all the time supplying jobs to the local community, meeting the demands of the marketplace, and producing profits for its stockholders. Reserve Mining seemed to meet all reasonable standards of corporate social responsibility: they conformed to the law, they caused no demonstrable harms, they provided jobs, they made a profit.

Conventional wisdom during this period was that the familiar categories of tort and liability law were sufficient for dealing with potential pollution problems. Business has a responsibility to not intentionally or negligently cause harm to others. If and when such harms do occur, business is required legally to compensate victims harmed by its actions. The threat of having to pay compensation is considered sufficient incentive for business to take reasonable steps to avoid causing harm.

An important aspect of this approach is that the burden of proof rests upon those who were harmed. Negligence law generally requires victims to prove three things: that they in fact were harmed, that the company acted negligently, and that this negligence caused the harm. Negligence itself can be understood in terms of acting in a way that a reasonable person could have foreseen would cause harm, or failing to act in a way that a reasonable person could have foreseen preventing harms. In this sense, the policy of negligence, liability, and compensation is a backward-looking approach. Society looks to the past at what business has done or has failed to do, assesses the harms that have occurred, and demands compensation as a payback for what happened in the past.

Beginning in the late 1960s, some evidence began to surface to suggest that Reserve Mining's discharge back into Lake Superior was harming fish and other lake life. Some residents also complained about the discharge, at first primarily on the aesthetic grounds that it was discoloring the lake. Some time later, studies found trace amounts of an asbestos-like mineral fiber in the drinking water that area cities drew from Lake Superior. This mineral was also found in the tailings discharged by Reserve Mining. On these grounds, several groups filed a lawsuit against Reserve Mining seeking to stop the company from discharging any more wastes into the lake.

As this case began in 1969, there were two legal avenues open to the critics. They could attempt to prove that the discharge was harmful, in which case there was a chance that the court would order it to end. They could also argue that Reserve Mining knew about, or should have known about, the potential danger and, thus, that Reserve was negligent in discharging the tailings. Legal relief for negligence would have included Reserve paying financial damages to compensate the victims for harms they incurred.

But while this case was being litigated, the political, social, and environmental landscape was changing. 1970 saw the creation of the Environmental Protection Agency (EPA) and passage of the first federal Clean Air Act. These were followed by the Clean Water Act (1972), the Pesticide Control Act (1972), and the Endangered Species Act (1973). These laws represented a clear shift in environmental policy away from the negligence and compensation model to more of a forward-looking approach of regulation and minimum standards. Rather than looking backward to determine what requires compensation, these policies looked to the future to establish standards that would prevent harms from occurring in the first place. Prevention rather than compensation became the public policy goal, with government regulations establishing minimum standards that, if met, would prevent harm.

Many consider the decision in the Reserve Mining case as the defining moment at which this change occurred. The scientific evidence surrounding the potential risks associated with the tailings was, and remains to this day, ambiguous. Nevertheless, the court ruled that the burden of proof was on Reserve Mining to show that the tailings were not harmful, rather than on citizens to show that they were. Without this proof, the court required the company to build a pipeline to pump the tailing several miles inland to a holding pond. The costs associated with this case came at the same time that the domestic steel industry declined in the face of foreign competition. Reserve Mining declared bankruptcy soon thereafter.

It might be tempting to think that few lessons can be drawn from this case. One could argue that Reserve Mining simply got caught in a changing social environment that its management either could not, or would not, anticipate. The legal landscape changed, and they were not able to keep pace. But this explanation is too simple. The same factors that explain the environmental shift of the early 1970s are at work for sustainability issues today. The change is occurring, and every business has very strong self-interest and ethical reasons to anticipate the change.

Consider the ethical rationale for a shift from a backward-looking negligence and compensation standard to a forward-looking regulatory and preventive standard. The compensation model adopts what is essentially a utilitarian ethic. Business practice that results in harms can be justified as long as the net social benefits (the social benefits of the product minus the compensation paid for the harm) are positive. Furthermore, the threat of compensation provides an incentive for avoiding harms. But there are good ethical reasons for rejecting this rationale.

First, it is ethically preferable to prevent harms from occurring rather than allowing them to occur and then seeking to compensate. This is particularly true when the harms involve such goods as health and safety. Compensation may be a good justice model for financial harms, but it is an offensive model for personal harms. Individual rights to health and safety should not be sacrificed merely for a net increase in overall social benefit. Illness or death caused by exposure to toxic wastes, for example, is not something for which money can compensate.

Second, the compensation model does not provide a reliable incentive to prevent harm. In fact, it may well provide an incentive for business to rely on a cost-benefit calculation when deciding what risks they should take. Ford Motor Company's economic calculations concerning potential liabilities that might arise from the dangerous Pinto gas tank is an example that comes to mind. But similar calculations occur in every liability insurance decision. The costs of potential compensation can be built into the original price and, effectively, create a license to harm. If a business, or its insurance company, determines that it can afford to pay compensation, there is every incentive to allow the harm to occur. Thus, compensation can function as a license to harm; anyone willing to pay the price can cause the harm.

Other reasons are particularly applicable to environmental concerns. The loss of many environmental and ecological benefits simply cannot be compensated. No compensation can make up for a lost species, a habitat, a native prairie, a wilderness area. As represented by Julian Simon, conventional economic wisdom interprets resources in terms of their uses and, therefore, assumes that we can always find substitutes for any given resource. This makes it easy to conclude that compensation for lost resources is always possible. To compensate for the loss of one resource, one simply provides a substitute. But if, instead, one understands that the value of many natural objects is not exhausted by the uses to which they are put, compensation for that loss is not possible. Put another way, one can compensate for the loss of an object's instrumental value, but one cannot compensate for loss of its intrinsic value. If something has intrinsic value, by definition, any substitute would not have the same intrinsic value.

Furthermore, many environmental and ecological harms are long-term. The infamous Love Canal was a case in point. Seepage of toxic chemicals buried at an onsite storage and waste dump occurred many years after the fact and well after the firm that originally disposed of them was no longer in business. Compensation was simply impossible in this case. Imagine a leak of nuclear wastes occurring 100 or 1000 years in the future. Who would be held liable? Who would pay damages? Future payouts provide present generation businesses with, at best, greatly discounted reasons to improve storage or eliminate waste today.

Finally, many environmental and ecological harms are also cumulative. No single firm is liable for the greenhouse gas emissions that bring about global warming. No single firm will be responsible for the groundwater contamination. No single firm is responsible for the rising incidence of allergies, cancers, and asthma brought about by exposure to toxic chemicals. Pollution from a single automobile or even a single power plant may not make much of a difference to global warming, but pollution from the entire industry does.

Similar considerations convinced courts and legislatures in the 1970s that a more forward-looking standard was needed to regulate pollution and the disposal of the wastes of production. Given this history, there is good reason to think that society will continue in the direction begun with Reserve Mining. Society, through the courts and legislatures, not only will demand that business be held liable for harms caused by the by-products of their production, but will continue to expect business to meet minimum safety and environmental standards before bringing a product to market. There is good reason for future public policy to move toward standards of minimal emissions and pollution for nontoxic wastes, and a zero-tolerance standard for toxic wastes and pollution. The emerging standards of "take-back" legislation throughout the European Union provide another example of society's changing expectations concerning business's responsibility for the wastes created by its products. Businesses that do not anticipate these changes and act accordingly may, like Reserve Mining, face an unsympathetic court and public in the future.

Life-Cycle Responsibility, Dematerialization, and Sustainable Energy Use

If pollution and waste lie at one side of the production process, resources and materials that go into products lie on the other. Once again, conventional wisdom, represented by Julian Simon's claim that resources are infinite, denies that there is a problem with the supply of resources. What was identified in Chapter Five as the *weak sustainability thesis* holds that as long as substitutes exist, any product is sustainable. If this were true, business would have no responsibility for creating sustainable products. But, to the degree that this is not true, and to the degree that business can foresee the harmful consequences of creating unsustainable products, business does have a responsibility to anticipate and prevent problems by designing and creating sustainable products.

Three trends in production that are likely to follow from this are worth considering in more detail. First, business should be expected to take responsibility throughout the entire life cycle of its products. A process called *life-cycle management* entails business accepting stewardship and managing products throughout their entire life cycle, including a "take-back" commitment. Second, business's liability for the materials used in products is likely to result in a movement toward dematerialization. Third, business should anticipate greater responsibility for the type of energy used in its production process.

The concept of life-cycle responsibility holds that business can be held liable for any harms caused by a product at any point in that product's life cycle. An ethical case can be made for the claim that when a business chooses to manufacture a product and bring it into the marketplace, it assumes a responsibility for that product that cannot be relinquished simply because someone else has purchased it. The implication is that a business that creates a product must take responsibility for managing its entire life.[3]

Life-cycle management is a tool that has its roots in pollution prevention strategies. Once business recognized that it would be held liable for harms caused downstream by its pollutants, an incentive was created to prevent the harms by reducing pollution upstream at its sources. Life-cycle management is most easily done within firms that are vertically integrated. The very concept of vertical integration, familiar throughout the business management literature, demonstrates that many businesses already control many of the life cycles of products. Life-cycle responsibility simply draws out the ethical implications of this fact and acknowledges that where business exercises control, it bears responsibility.

The Interface story again provides a good illustration of how life-cycle management can effect profound changes throughout a corporation. CEO Ray Anderson explained how much of his own motivation for transforming

Interface came from the recognition that a vast amount of Interface carpeting ended up in landfills. Despite the fact that Interface was diligent in obeying all environmental laws, it estimated that some 5 billion tons of Interface carpeting is buried within landfills. Carpet wastes can be toxic and are non-biodegradable. Used carpeting was not disposed of; it was only hidden beneath the surface of municipal landfills and dumps. Once Interface decided to take responsibility for the end-of-life of its products, the entire nature of the business changed.

Imagine a person who believed that he was adequately cleaning his home by sweeping dirt under the carpet. Such a solution is only apparent and unsustainable over the long term. Once this is recognized, one must find ways to truly clean the house. Although one might begin to seek ways to dispose of the dirt permanently, one soon learns that the best approach is to eliminate the amount of dirt coming in in the first place. Life-cycle management, as Interface discovered, can profoundly change the way one does business.

The ethics of products liability law again offers supporting rationales for such changes. First, business should not assume that it foregoes responsibility whenever it sells a product. As witnessed in the development of products liability law within the United States, liability for harmful products is not transferred to a purchaser when the product itself is sold. Second, the negligence standard has always included an element of foreseeability. The law holds individuals and businesses liable for harms that a reasonable person could have foreseen occurring as a result of his or her actions. Growing awareness of the ecological and health harms caused by materials used in products virtually guarantees that future businesses will be judged negligent for failing to take steps to prevent easily foreseeable harms. Additionally, the law governing strict products liability suggests that even when business is not negligent, society is willing to hold it liable for harms caused by any product judged to be unreasonably harmful. Someone must be held accountable for harms done by unsustainable products, and fairness suggests that the business that placed such a product in the product stream is the most obvious candidate.

In many ways, contemporary products liability law already provides a basis for holding a business liable through the entire life cycle of its products. Early products liability law was governed by the privity of the contract standard in which producers' liability extended only to those with whom they had a direct contract. This changed with the 1916 case *MacPherson v. Buick*, in which an automobile manufacturer was held liable for damages suffered by a consumer, even though there was no direct contractual relationship between the consumer and manufacturer. This case established the legal precedent that liability for harms is not transferred with a transfer of ownership. The retailer who purchased the automobile from the manufacturer did not thereby assume responsibility for the product's safety. Courts reasoned that the manufacturer, and not the retailer or the consumer, was in the best position to ensure the safety of products. Manufacturers could be sued for negligent design, failing to inspect a product, negligent manufacture, or the failure to take any steps that reasonably could have been foreseen to prevent the harm.

A parallel can be made between twentieth-century products liability law and twenty-first century sustainability requirements. Designing, manufacturing, and selling a product today without considering the ecological costs involved throughout its entire life cycle is like designing, manufacturing, and selling a product in the past without considering its safety and health costs. As businesses in many localities throughout the United States have discovered, harmful and toxic products have a way of enduring. From dramatic cases such as Love Canal and Superfund sites to local landfills, governments at all levels are dealing with problems left behind by past business decisions. Failing to take steps now to prevent these harms will make it likely that a business will be found negligent in the future, even if the harms occur late in or even after the useful life expectancy of the product.

This negligence standard looks to the mental state of the producer, to what could have or should have been foreseen. Neglecting to do what could have reasonably been expected is the core idea of negligence. But the law has moved beyond even this standard with the doctrine of strict products liability. Under this policy, a firm can be held liable for damages caused by any product proven to be defective, regardless of what the producer could have foreseen. That is, even if the harm could not reasonably have been foreseen and steps therefore taken to prevent it, strict products liability holds business accountable for damages.

Three general ethical rationales have been offered to support this liability standard. First, the argument is made that even without negligence, businesses are still in the best position to take steps to prevent harms caused by their products. The strict products liability standard provides even greater incentive for business to design and manufacture safe products. Second, business is considered to be in the best position to pay for damages, if only by passing the costs on to consumers who use the product. In some ways, strict products liability is a method of internalizing externalities. Long-term and unanticipated costs of a product get internalized when producers are held accountable for paying them. Third, an argument is made from the principle of fairness. Some of the rules of market economics hold that entrepreneurial businesses take risks in the hopes of making a profit. Failing to hold businesses accountable for harms caused by their products diminishes business's risks by unfairly passing them on to those who suffer the harms.

As part of this life-cycle responsibility, business must begin a process of "dematerialization." Industrial ecologists are looking to dematerialization as an important step in the direction of sustainability. Dematerialization is a process of reducing the material use required for any given product or service. If we start with a standard economic understanding of the value of goods and service in terms of consumer satisfaction, dematerialization is the process of decreasing the amount of material resources that are required to produce a set unit of satisfaction. Dematerialization would aim to decrease both the amount and the rate at which material resources are used.

Business has tremendous opportunities to use dematerialization as a cost-cutting and marketing strategy. Dematerialization can involve a wide range of actions, including reducing product size, weight, and the amount of packaging, and increasing product life and range of uses. The information technology industry is a model for dematerialization as e-mail replaces physical mail, computers get faster and smaller, and computing services such as printing, fax, copying, and scanning get incorporated into single machines.[4] Hewlett-Packard, for example, is an industry leader in developing opportunities by which information technology creates less demand for physical products. The automobile industry has decreased the average weight of cars, despite the increased popularity of SUVs, by more than 30% during the last three decades of the twentieth century. The evolution of the music industry from vinyl records to eight-track tapes to cassettes tapes to CDs to digital players is another perfect example of this dematerialization process.

Dematerialization can also involve such practices as reduced fertilizer and pesticide use in agriculture. Many farmers now use global positioning satellite systems to more precisely identify crop areas in need of irrigation or fertilizers, thus using these resources only where and when necessary. Sensors that shut off appliances when not in use, timers aimed at reducing electricity usage, and hybrid technologies in automobiles that shift to battery power when gasoline power is inefficient, are also all part of a movement toward dematerialization.

At first glance, it might appear that dematerialization is an obvious strategy for creating efficiencies. Doing more with less would seem a clear means for reducing costs and increasing revenues. But this is not always the case. As the fast-food industry so clearly understands, economies of scale can show that doing the same with more may be the road to increased revenues. Super-sized portions, two-for-one specials, and all-you-can-eat buffets increase revenues per unit of product—the very opposite of dematerialization. Nevertheless, in most instances, dematerialization will serve two of the three goals of sustainability. It is a process that should be both financially and ecologically beneficial.

Besides materials, energy is the other major factor that goes into the production process. Unquestionably, energy use is at the heart of sustainable business practice. Global energy use at present, with its heavy reliance on fossil fuels and nuclear power, is a major cause of ecological damage. Few believe that fossil fuels and nuclear power are a part of a long-term sustainable energy policy. At best, these energy sources will require significant safeguards and technological improvements to be a part of a transition toward sustainability. Long-term, they will need to be replaced as sources for the energy business requires.[5]

As suggested by the diagram on page 57, only solar energy provides new energy input into the earth's biosphere. Solar energy, directly in the form of heat energy absorbed through solar panels or indirectly through wind energy, is the most sustainable long-term energy source. Fuel cells, powered by hydrogen produced through solar and wind power, hold great promise for localized distributed electric power generation. Geothermal, tidal, and some hydro-powered energy sources also have long-term potential. Until such energy sources are more readily available, we might have to rely on technologies to create cleaner and more benign uses of fossil fuels. Hybrid electric and internal combustion engines for automobiles, ultra-clean sulfur-free diesel fuel for truck and heavy machinery, coal-to-liquid, and coal-to-gas technologies can decrease pollution from otherwise unsustainable fossil fuels.

In Chapter Six, the Natural Step funnel metaphor was introduced, which describes the converging lines of resource availability and societal demand for resources. This metaphor was designed to help business visualize what would be necessary to attain sustainability at a time early enough that there will be more options available to meet that goal. Perhaps nowhere is this metaphor better modeled than in the energy sector. There is strong evidence suggesting that availability and acceptability of fossil fuel energy resources are decreasing significantly. At the same time, global demand for those resources, especially from China, India, and other developing countries, is increasing significantly.

The recognition of this convergence was at the center of a recent call from the Chairman and CEO of Chevron-Texaco for changes in U.S. energy policy. In a speech delivered in February 2005, David J. O'Reilly claimed that we are now in the midst of what he called a "new energy equation."

> The most visible element of this new equation is that relative to demand, oil is no longer in plentiful supply. The time when we could count on cheap oil and even cheaper natural gas is clearly ending. Why is this happening now? . . . *Demand from Asia is one fundamental reason* for this new age of more volatile and higher prices. The Chinese economy alone is a roaring engine whose thirst for oil grew by more than 15 percent last year and will double its need for imported oil between 2003 and 2010—just seven years. This new Asian demand is reshaping the marketplace. And we're seeing the center of gravity of global petroleum markets shift to Asia and, in particular, to China and India. . . . *But demand isn't the only factor at play. Simply put, the era of easy access to energy is over.* In part, this is because we are experiencing the convergence of geological difficulty with geopolitical instability. Although political turmoil and social unrest are less likely to affect long-term supplies, the psychological effect of those factors can clearly have an impact on world oil markets, which are already running at razor-thin margins of capacity. Many of the world's big production fields are maturing just as demand is increasing. The U.S. Geological Survey estimates the world will have consumed one-half of its existing conventional oil base by 2030. Increasingly, future supplies will have to be found in ultradeep water and other

remote areas, development projects that will ultimately require new technology and trillions of dollars of investment in new infrastructure.[6] [emphasis added]

In Chapter One, we saw a political response to such factors in the energy policy described by U.S. Vice President Richard Cheney. Given the convergence of the downward-sloping line of energy availability and the upward-sloping line of global demand, Cheney argued that government must move quickly and aggressively to create policies to help meet that demand, that is, increase the availability of energy resources and thereby decrease the slope of the resource line. The role of business was notably absent in the Vice President's description of the present situation. In the remainder of this chapter, let us reflect on the role of business in this situation.

At first glance, one might think of business as belonging on the production side of the Vice President's equation. Consumers are demanding ever-increasing amounts of energy, and government policy should encourage production to meet that demand. Ordinarily, we assume that it is the role of business to produce what is demanded by consumers. This, of course, is true if we are thinking of energy companies such as the oil, natural gas, coal, and nuclear industries. But for every business that produces energy that is sold in the marketplace, there are countless other businesses that demand energy as consumers. We turn now to the role of businesses as consumers, and specifically to the responsibility of businesses to demand sustainable products from their suppliers.

BUSINESSES AS CONSUMERS: SUPPLY-CHAIN RESPONSIBILITY

In recent years, public attention has focused on the responsibility of businesses for the actions of their supply-chain, particularly concerning two issues. Food and agricultural businesses have been challenged concerning the presence of genetically modified organisms in the food supply, and retail and textile industries have been challenged regarding sweatshop working conditions in their supply chain. In both situations, the initial reply of the businesses involved was to deny responsibility for the actions of their suppliers. In both situations, that defense quickly collapsed in the face of public pressure. A strong ethical case can be made for the claim that businesses can be held responsible for the practices of their suppliers.

Ordinarily, we do not hold a person responsible for the actions of someone else. Assuming that the other person is an autonomous agent, we believe that each person is responsible for his or her actions. But this is not always the case. For example, we hold parents responsible for the actions of their children. Thus, the ethical and philosophical challenge is to determine exactly when and under what conditions doing so is reasonable.

Let us begin by first reflecting on the understanding of consumer responsibility that is implicit in conventional economic wisdom. In an essay cited previously, philosopher Norman Bowie argued that the environmental responsibilities of businesses were exhausted by the duties to obey the law and respect the minimum moral obligation of causing no harm. In Bowie's view, society gets two opportunities to direct business toward sustainable ends. First, as citizens, individuals have the opportunity to support laws that would require business to adopt sustainable practices. Second, as consumers, we have the opportunity to demand sustainable products from business. Besides legal requirements and consumer demand, business has no special environmental responsibility. Thus, Bowie locates the responsibility for environmentally safe products with individual consumers/citizens.

Vice President Cheney, likewise, locates the responsibility for energy policy with consumers. Consumer demand is a given, and the responsibility of government is to respond to that demand. In the Vice President's words, "conservation may be a sign of personal virtue, but it is not a sufficient basis for a sound, comprehensive energy policy."[7]

These two views share a common philosophical assumption. Producers and suppliers, whether they are private businesses or government agencies, are relatively passive in their role of meeting consumer demand. Ethically, their role is limited by the demands placed on them by others. Asking producers and suppliers to do otherwise is to ask them to take unreasonable risks.

Although it is easy to think of consumers solely in terms of individual human beings, it would be a mistake to do so. In common situations, we think of a consumer as the person who walks into a big-box retail outlet, an automobile showroom, or stands at the gas pump refueling a private car. But as the case of such giant retailers as Wal-Mart has so clearly demonstrated in recent years, retail businesses exercise tremendous control and influence over both their suppliers and the individual consumers who ostensibly make demands on them. If we hold individual consumers responsible for the choices they make in the marketplace, as conventional economic wisdom would have us do, then we must hold individual businesses equally responsible for the choices they make in the wholesale and supply-chain marketplace.

Consider the example of NatureWorks, a company that manufactures plastics derived from corn and other biological products.[8] The plastic industry today relies on oil to produce the 450 billion pounds of plastics every year. None of this plastic is biodegradable, and most ends up in landfills. NatureWorks' plastic, designed at this point primarily for use in bottles and containers, is produced by bacteria that feed on organic matter. Although polylactic acid (PLA) plastic is biodegradable at high temperatures and in moist settings, it performs very comparably to oil-based plastics in normal situations. Thus, NatureWorks would appear to have a product that is comparable to an unsustainable product in terms of costs and performance and outperforms oil-based plastics on environmental grounds. Nevertheless, NatureWorks has struggled to gain business.

Imagine the implications if a major business that relies on plastic containers, a business such as Procter & Gamble or Coca-Cola, or any major supermarket chain, took leadership and required its suppliers to purchase corn-based plastics. The purchasing power of major businesses creates both the opportunity and the responsibility to move suppliers toward a more sustainable future.

There is a legal parallel to the idea that a business should be held responsible for the actions of its suppliers. The doctrine of *respondeat superior*, Latin for "let the master answer," holds a principal (e.g., an employer) responsible for the actions of an agent (e.g., an employee) when that agent is acting in the ordinary course of his or her duties to the principal.[9] Thus, in the standard example, an employer can be held liable for damages caused by an accident involving an employee driving the company car on company business.

The justification for doing what might otherwise be considered unfair is that the agent is acting on the principal's behalf, at the principal's direction, and that the principal has direct influence over the agent's actions. Thus, if someone is doing something for you, at your direction, and under your influence, then you must take at least some responsibility for his or her actions. Most of the ethical rationale for the responsibility of business for the actions of its suppliers stems from two of these conditions: suppliers often act at the direction of business, and business often exercises significant influence over the actions of its suppliers. But before considering these two aspects, let us consider the simple case of business as consumer.

In many situations, a business is much like an individual consumer in the sense that it can neither directly nor significantly influence the acts of those from whom it purchases goods and services. An individual business, like an individual consumer, may have little choice concerning the source of the electricity it purchases, for example. Like individual consumers, business's choice is limited by what is available at a competitive price in the marketplace. Individual consumers may have limited ability to influence the market for sustainable products. Nevertheless, we can ask that consumers express their desire, purchase such products when available, and perhaps even be willing to pay a premium for them. We can also expect consumers to lobby not only business but also government to make such products available. Thus, we can expect individual businesses to play a role in creating a market for sustainable products in much the same way that we can expect individual consumers to do so.

But, in many ways business is not at all like an ordinary, individual consumer. The two major differences provide a framework for the remainder of this chapter. First, the goods and services supplied to a business are often goods and services designed and produced at the direction of and expressly for the business. Second, much of business purchasing occurs in bulk quantities that give businesses significant influence over their design and manufacture. Again, consider the example of what a major corporation such as Procter and Gamble or Coke could do for the biodegradable plastic industry. One major client could create the market for a business that produces sustainable products. These two factors create a strong case for claiming considerable business responsibility for the creation of sustainable products.

Consider an example cited by McDonough and Braungart and mentioned in the previous chapter. DesignTex is a U.S. company that specializes in the design of commercial fabrics, many used in the manufacture of upholstery for office furnishings. Beginning in the 1990s, DesignTex executives began looking for ways to create more environmentally friendly fabrics, recognizing that some of the dyes and synthetic materials used to manufacture their fabrics might be environmentally harmful. DesignTex worked with dozens of mills throughout the world to manufacture their products and began soliciting advice and samples from their suppliers in the hope of finding a more sustainable product. Initially, no textile mills had the type of sustainable product DesignTex sought.

At the same time, one of their suppliers, the Swiss firm Rohner Textil, was experiencing its own environmental problems. Some of the wastes from Rohner's mill had been classified as toxic by local environmental authorities, and Rohner was under a legal mandate to clean up its effluents. Textile manufacturing involves dyes, bleaches, glues, plastics, and a variety of chemicals. Synthetic fibers were manufactured from petrochemicals, and even natural fibers such as cotton and wool were found to contain traces of pesticides. Rohner faced major challenges in disposing the by-products of its manufacturing. Thus, DesignTex's marketplace demands created the incentive and opportunity for Rohner to create sustainable fabric and dyes.

Both firms worked with McDonough and Braungart to design and develop a fabric that would be ecologically sustainable but still meet the performance and aesthetic demands of the market. They soon encountered a familiar difficulty: there was no market for safe and ecologically benign dyes that they could turn to for supplies. DesignTex and Rohner wanted to purchase sustainable products, but nobody had them to sell. Dye manufacturers were unwilling to disclose the ingredients in their products and were suspicious of any request to analyze and evaluate them on environmental grounds.

Examples such as NatureWorks and DesignTex highlight the simplicity of the consumer-producer model that dominates many discussions of business responsibility. Who is the consumer of biodegradable plastics or environmentally safe fabric dyes? Certainly one way to influence sustainable production is through the demands of the ultimate individual consumer who purchases a bottle of water or a piece of office furniture. But, throughout an entire supply chain, there are consumers and producers, buyers and sellers, each able to influence the decisions of others up and down the supply chain. A major bottler of soft drinks or manufacturer of office furniture can demand sustainable products from its suppliers while also marketing those products in ways that inform and educate end consumers. What may be an ethical responsibility on one side, is a business opportunity on the other.

Endnotes

1 I rely here on "Chemical Contaminants in Breast Milk and Their Impacts on Children's Health: An Overview," Philip J. Landrigan et al. *Environmental Health Perspectives* Volume 110, Number 6, June 2002, accessible at: http://ehp.niehs.nih .gov/members/2002/110pA313-A315landrigan/landrigan-full.html.

2 See McDonough Braungart Design Chemistry (MBDC), available at: http://www .mbdc.com/c2c_mbdp.htm.

3 Significant work on life-cycle management is being done by the United Nations Environment Progamme, http://www.uneptie.org/pc/sustain/lcinitiative/

4 "Sustainability and Dematerialization at Hewlett Packard," by David Hudson and Lynelle Preston, *Ants, Galileo, and Gandhi: Designing the Future of Business through Nature, Genius, and Compassion*, Sissel Waage, ed. (Sheffield, U.K, Greenleaf Publishing, 2003), pp. 82–92.

5 A strong case can be made for the claim that world oil production already is at, or has passed, its peak. As early as the 1950s, geophysicist M. King Hubbert formulated a hypothesis concerning a point of maximum production, known as Hubbert Peak, for any resource. Hubbert's hypothesis included the claim that the production peak occurred at the midpoint of the depletion of a resource. Many geologists and oil engineers believe that the world has already hit Hubbert's peak for oil production. A helpful source for pursuing this claim can be found at http://www.hubbertpeak.com/.

6 "U.S. Energy Policy: A Declaration of Interdependence," remarks by David J. O'Reilly, Chairman and CEO, Chevron-Texaco Corporation. Keynote address to the 24th annual CERAWeek Conference, Houston, Texas February 15, 2005 available on the Chevron-Texaco website: http://www.chevrontexaco.com/news/ speeches/2005/2005-02-15_oreilly.asp.

7 Vice President Richard Cheney, speech to the Associated Press annual meeting, Toronto. May 5, 2001.

8 This account of NatureWorks is taken from *"Plastic Fantastic,"* by Elizabeth MacDonald, *Forbes* March 28, 2005 and a lecture delivered by Kathleen Bader, CEO of NatureWorks, as the "Business and Environmental Sustainability" conference, University of Minnesota Carlson School of Management, April 14, 2005.

9 This parallel is explained in Michael Santoro, *"Profits and Principles: Global Capitalism and Human Rights in China,"* (Ithaca: Cornell University Press, 2000), p. 161 and is cited as well by Denis Arnold and Norman Bowie, *"Sweatshops and Respects for Persons,"* Business Ethics Quarterly, Vol. 13, No. 2 (2003) 221–242.

chapter eight

Sustainable Consumption

INTRODUCTION

In Chapter Two, a formula was introduced that is widely used in thinking about environmental impact: $I = PAT$. Environmental impact (I) is a product of population (P), consumption per capita, or affluence (A), and technology (T). Within this context, the consumerist lifestyle has been particularly criticized. People in consumer-driven societies use proportionately higher percentages of the earth resources, and generate proportionately higher percentages of wastes and pollution, than do the less affluent people of the world. These facts raise a number of important ethical questions: Why do people consume *what* they do, *how* they do, and *as much* as they do? Do people living in the industrialized world consume too much? Are there alternative consumption patterns that would be more sustainable? If the consumerist lifestyle cannot be available to all, is it fair that it is enjoyed only by those in the developed world?

As business begins to address sustainability concerns, it might seem that consumerism lies beyond what we can reasonably ask business to address. Expecting business to take responsibility, or holding business liable, for the consequences of consumer choice seems unreasonable and unfair. First, what would seem to be the primary alternatives to consumerism—movements such as voluntary simplicity and virtues like frugality and thrift—run counter to business's interests in selling more products. If consumers stop consuming, business loses. If consumers consume less, the economy enters a recession, and everyone suffers. Thus, it would seem that asking business to discourage consumption is asking it to put its own survival in jeopardy. Second, consumer demand—the motivating force behind consumerism—seems beyond the scope of business's ethical responsibilities. Business responds to the market after all, it does not create the market. If consumers make environmentally bad decisions, the fault should lie with individual consumers, not with business.

Nevertheless, I would like to suggest that business has more of a responsibility for consumer behavior and consumption patterns than might first appear. A sustainable business must address the issue of consumption head-on. Business must take responsibility both for the role it plays in shaping consumer demand and for the choices available to fill that demand. Furthermore, sustainable consumerism can present business with as many opportunities as barriers and managers who miss such opportunities fail all their stakeholders. But first, it will help if we review the ethics of modern consumerism.

SUSTAINABLE CONSUMPTION

In Chapter Two, some of the most troubling trends affecting the present state of the earth's biosphere are described. The formula, $I = PAT$, implies that consumption patterns, particularly those found in the United States and other developed and industrialized societies, have a profound negative impact on the biosphere.

Many observers dispute the more pessimistic conclusions drawn from these patterns of consumption. Most of these challenges mirror responses to the criticisms of economic growth discussed previously. Consumption is not a problem, and "over-consumption" is a misnomer, because economic growth can continue indefinitely. Because we can continue to grow, we can continue to consume. Furthermore, because growth is good, consumption also is good.

To begin evaluating these claims, let us reflect on various meanings of consumption. In standard economic usage, consumption refers to any economic value or income that is spent rather than saved. Consumption is what is measured by spending. On this model, value gets added in the production process and used in the consumption process. Consumption in the aggregate is what is measured by the Gross National Product (GDP) and thus, by definition, consumption can increase as long as spending increases. In this specialized economic sense, consumer goods typically are divided into durable goods, nondurable goods, and services. Durable goods are products that last a long time (hopefully) such as a house, a car, furniture. Nondurable goods are those that have a shorter lifespan, such as a hamburger, the morning newspaper, and gasoline. Services, such as health care, video rentals, insurance, a mortgage, and financial advice, refer to spending for the value provided by an activity rather than by a product or commodity. Accordingly, in this economic sense, I can be said to consume my refrigerator when I purchase it, a hamburger when I eat it, a movie when I rent the video, and advice when I speak to my broker, doctor, or lawyer. To help us stay clear, I will identify this specialized economic sense as consumption$_1$.

In what is perhaps a more ordinary usage, "consumption" refers to something being used up or depleted. Common dictionaries often define the verb *to consume* in terms of destroying something by using it, or in terms of decomposing or wasting away. "Consumption" in this sense refers to a process of decay in which what is consumed no longer exists, or exists only in a depleted and worn-out form. In this sense, I consume the hamburger when I eat and digest it, not simply when I purchase it. As another often quoted example, the disease tuberculosis was for many years referred to simply as "consumption."

This meaning of consumption also seems to parallel the ecological economists' discussions about entropy. When we consume something, we inevitably convert its form of matter/energy from a low- to a high entropy state. Consumption unavoidably decays the available uses of matter/energy. To distinguish this understanding from the economic meaning of consumption, I will identify this as consumption$_2$.

Given these varied meanings, it is not surprising that debates about the ethics of consumption can be bewildering even to some of its participants. In the narrow economic sense, the value that is consumed is not lost or destroyed in the process. This can be seen particularly well in the case of services. The amount or quality of my doctor's advice is not destroyed or diminished by the fact that I have consumed some of it. But in a more common sense, anything consumed is diminished. What one side sees as obviously true, another sees as obviously false.

But, there are lessons to be learned from this dispute. Certainly, some products, once consumed, are degraded in such a way that they are forever lost for human use. The natural gas that I consume as heat to keep my home warm is degraded in that process into useless by-products, such as waste heat, carbon dioxide, and other pollutants. Once I take the heat value from that gas, there is little left that is useful. Indeed, the very concept of waste, and the complementary environmentalist advice to reuse and recycle, suggests that we often do not fully degrade what we use, or to put it differently, we often do not fully consume$_2$ what we consume$_1$.

Given this, how might we define sustainable consumption? Consistent with the standard definition of sustainable development, the United Nations has characterized sustainable consumption as "Sustainable consumption includes meeting the needs of present and future generations for goods and services in ways that are economically, socially and environmentally sustainable" (United Nations, 1995). Another definition describes sustainable consumption as "the use of services and related products which respond to basic needs and bring a better quality of life while minimizing the use of natural resources and toxic materials as well as the emissions of waste and pollutants over the life cycle so as not to jeopardize the needs of future generations."[1] Yet another definition defines sustainable consumption as

> "the selection, use, and disposal of products and services in a way that conserves energy and materials, minimizes the depletion of natural resources, avoids toxic and hazardous substances, and optimizes the quality of life of consumers and workers throughout the life cycle of the products or services ("from cradle to cradle"). Like sustainable production, sustainable consumption involves meeting present needs without compromising the capacity of future generations to do the same. Examples of sustainable consumption practices include: the sharing,

repair, and reuse of products; the use of durable, long-lasting, and upgradable products; and the use of products whose constituent materials are renewable or replenishable."[2]

More simply, "sustainable consumption" can be defined as consumption that does not use up, deplete, or diminish the available supply of resources, or as consumption that is not consumption.

We can thus describe a range of positions concerning sustainable consumption. At one extreme is the view described in Chapter Three and represented by Julian Simon. The resources that go into production are effectively infinite because what is consumed is the use value of the resources, and this use value is infinite. Price pressure caused by diminishing supply will provide incentives to find substitutes for any resource before it is fully consumed. Thus, consumption, like resources and economic growth, can continue indefinitely. From this perspective, consumption is the appropriate understanding and consumption is a misnomer. Although particular consumption types and patterns may not be sustainable, consumption itself in the aggregate is.

At the other extreme would be a position that concludes that all economic consumption is also consumption and that, therefore, all consumption degrades resources and increases entropy. If this is so, then sustainable consumption is an ideal that cannot be realized in practice. The ideal of sustainable consumption provides more of a target at which consumption should aim or a standard by which we can judge consumption patterns as more or less sustainable.

Between these extremes are a range of alternatives in which particular consumption patterns are more or less sustainable. Some consumption, one thinks here of such commodities as oil and gas or natural resources such as wetlands, and ocean fish species, necessarily diminishes the supply and degrades the usable value. But, this discussion also suggests a direction for future consumption patterns, a direction that echoes previous discussions of the service-and-flow business model. Following standard economic definitions, durable and nondurable goods clearly get used up and depleted by the act of consumption, but economic services may not. This suggests that consumption of services is more likely to be sustainable over the long-term than consumption of products and commodities. If this is so, we have one direction in which environmentally responsible business can develop. Business ought to seek ways to replace the sale of products and commodities with services.

Another alternative to the utilitarian frugality of voluntary simplicity might emphasize the quality rather than quantity of consumption. Much of the discussion of sustainable consumption focuses on how much we consume: Is it "too much" to be sustainable? But a complementary approach would emphasize the quality of what we consume. One does not sacrifice by consuming less if what one consumes is better. What we might call "smart consumption" or "good consumption" recognizes that many good reasons there are to consume and seeks to distinguish good from bad consumption. Just as the alternative to unfettered economic growth is not "no growth" but "smart growth," the alternative to unfettered consumption is not no consumption, but smart consumption.

Thus, sustainable consumption need not require consumers simply to consume less. Consuming services rather than products, and consuming better rather than more, are part of a more sustainable economy. I suggest that business has a role to play in each of these tasks. To make good on the claim that business has an ethical responsibility to address issues of consumerism, however, two previous topics must be addressed. We need to explain exactly what the problem of consumption is. Why should present consumption patterns be changed? Also, we would need to identify the causes of present consumption patterns if business is to be expected to bring about a change. We turn now to these two topics.

CONSUMPTION: TOO MUCH OF A GOOD THING?

Implicit in most environmental discussions of consumption is the belief that present consumption patterns within most of the industrial world consume too much of the Earth's resources. But do we consume too much? The only reasonable answer to this general question is: It depends. It depends on to whom "we" refers, what is being "consumed," and what harm is implied by the "too much."

Let us begin by comparing consumption patterns among the world's rich and poor. One estimate suggests that worldwide, 1.2 billion people live on less than $1 a day, and 2.8 billion people live on less than $2 a day. A similar estimate suggests that close to 4 billion people live on the equivalent of $2 per day.[3] In contrast, 12% of the world's population who live in North America and Western Europe account for 60% of worldwide consumer expenditures. The wealthiest 25% of the world's population consumes 58% of the energy, 45% of the meat and fish, 84% of the paper, and 87% of the vehicles, and accounts for 86% of the total private consumer expenditures. In contrast, the world's poorest 25% consumes 24% of the energy, 5% of the meat and fish, 1% of the paper, and less than 1% of the vehicles, and accounts for only 1.3% of the total private consumer expenditures. More than one-third of the world's population, approximately 2 billion people, lives in sub-Saharan Africa and south Asia. Combined, they account for less than 4% of the total worldwide consumption expenditures.[4]

The United States alone, with 5% of the world's population, consumes 25% of the annual fossil fuel use. From 1975 to 1999, the size of the average U.S. household declined from 2.94 to 2.61 people, but the size of the average home increased from 1900 square feet to more than 2300 square feet. The size of the average American home in the 1950s was 900 square feet, the same size as the typical three-car garage built in 2000.[5]

But even within developed economies, not everyone consumes equally. More than 30 million Americans, 10% of the United States population, live below the poverty line and struggle for access to food, housing, and health care. Although home size has increased, it has been estimated that some 2 million Americans, 40% of whom are in family groups, are homeless. Similar disparities, some even more greatly exaggerated, occur in every society in both the developed and developing world.

Thus, we can categorize the "we" as members of the consumer class who are free from the daily struggles to attain adequate food, shelter, and health care. The consumer class can be identified as those people who have their needs met and for whom such products as telephones, televisions, and computers are facts of daily life. In a 2004 report, Worldwatch Institute estimates this class as 1.7 billion people worldwide, almost half of whom now live in developing countries.

In what sense, then, might this be "too much"? A case can be made that the consumption patterns of this consumer class is too much in three distinct ways: such consumption is causing serious harm to the Earth's biosphere and, therefore, is "too much" environmentally and ecologically; such consumption is an unjust distribution of Earth's resources and is, therefore, "too much" ethically; and such consumption goes against our own best interests and is, therefore, "too much" as a matter of prudence.

In Chapter Two, numerous threats presently facing the Earth's biosphere were presented. The biosphere clearly is stressed by the productivity of modern agriculture, fishing, and animal farming, mining, timber harvest, and so forth. Because this productivity after all is driven by consumer demand, we cannot be sanguine about the environmental effects of consumption. However, we have also reviewed the views of such market defenders as Julian Simon who argued that resources are infinite, and, therefore, we can never consume too much. Ultimately, the question of whether we consume too much on environmental grounds comes down to the question of how serious one thinks the problem of environmental destruction is. Rather than rehearse that entire argument here, I would like to focus on only two specific issues: global climate change and loss of biodiversity.

The argument of market defenders is that market forces will work toward an equilibrium that will attain an optimal level of pollution or resource depletion. Thus, as we pollute the atmosphere and water, or deplete resources, the scarcity of these goods will result in a price rise that will both lower demand and provide an incentive for substitutes. The two specific issues to take notice of are the time lag between the increasing scarcity of such resources, and the question of whether there are substitutes for everything.

Consider the case of greenhouse gases. One fundamental "resource" that is used up in the consumption of fossil fuels is the atmosphere's capacity to absorb greenhouse gases. Consider how the market would signal an increasing scarcity of this resource. We would get signals that an increase in greenhouse gases is having dangerous effects on the global climate: temperatures are rising, rain patterns are changing, the intensity of tropical storms is increasing, droughts are occurring, and so forth. Imagine that the science and facts become undisputed: an increase in CO_2 and other greenhouse gas emissions is responsible for these threats. Imagine that the entire world agreed today that we had reached the optimal level of atmospheric greenhouse gas pollution. Even if consumption patterns changed overnight, it would not be fast enough to prevent serious harm. Changing atmosphere and climate is, like a giant ocean liner underway, not something that can be stopped instantly. By the time market forces produce the information to signal that climate change is occurring, we will already have overshot the point in time that we could have changed to prevent harm.

This time lag between when scarcity first begins to occur and when market forces change in reaction to it may seem trivial when the scarce resource is copper, chrome, nickel, tin, and tungsten (as in Simon's bet with Ehrlich), but it is not trivial when the resource is the atmosphere. A similar point could be made for such "resources" as endangered plant and animal species, the Earth's storage capacity for nuclear wastes, aquifers, the ocean's capacity to absorb hypoxia-producing pollutants, the ozone's layer's capacity to absorb ozone-depleting chemicals, and the food-chain's capacity to absorb pesticides and herbicides.

A second issue addresses my use of scare quotes around the word "resources" in the preceding paragraphs. In one sense, natural resources simply are those objects that have a use to us. They are, in this way, instrumentally valuable. But more generally, resources refer to any natural object, including endangered plant and animal species, which, many believe, have an intrinsic value. When the value of an object lies exclusively in the ways in which it can be used, the possibility of finding a substitute is always open. But if the value of something is intrinsic rather than merely instrumental, by definition there can be no substitute. Viewed as a resource with mere instrumental value, humans may well be capable of finding substitutes for plant and animal species. If the swordfish becomes extinct, we can fulfill our protein needs in other ways. But if the swordfish becomes extinct, its intrinsic value will be lost forever. There is no substitute. Thus, consumption that uses up plant and animal species would be consuming too much in the sense that it is consuming irreplaceable life forms.

A second way in which we can be said to be consuming too much is that consumption patterns constitute an unjust or unfair allocation of scarce resources. Thus, we can be said to be consuming too much in an ethical sense. Perhaps the most insightful commentary on this issue can be found in

John Locke's classic justification of private property rights. Locke argued that private ownership of property could be ethically justified on various grounds, including personal liberty, autonomy, utility, and fairness. But, Locke argued, this justification was valid only if the equal rights of others were not violated in the process. Locke's famous caveat was that private property was ethically justified as long as "as much and as good" was left in common—as long as my possession of private property did not prevent others from an equal opportunity to likewise come to possess private property.

Perhaps this is the most fundamental ethical challenge to the consumption patterns of the contemporary consumer class. Resources spent on consumer goods are resources not spent on essential goods elsewhere. Juliet Shor points to this misallocation in the following:

> "Americans spend more on cosmetics every year (in excess of $8 billion) than the extra expenditure needed to bring universal access to basic education to all the children in the developing world. The U.S. and Europe together spend $17 billion a year on pet foods, more than the $13 billion increment it would cost to ensure basic health and nutrition around the world."[6]

We consume too much if the capital, labor, and natural resources allocated to satisfy the consumer demand for inconsequential and frivolous products is thereby denied to the production of nontrivial products for the poor.

The third general way in which we can be said to consume too much is in terms of our own best interests. Much of the economic and business discussion about consumption focuses on the question of what consumption does for us. What are the goods and services provided for consumers in the marketplace? From the perspective of the conventional economic and business wisdom, consumption is good if it on balance does good things *for* us. But an equally important question is what consumption does *to* us.[7] What type of people do we become when we conform to the consumer lifestyle? What kind of person is the "consumer" of modern consumer-oriented society? What kind of children do we raise, what kind of families do we create, in a consumerist culture?

The U.S. Centers for Disease Control and Prevention (CDC) reports that obesity is the fastest growing health threat in the United States, approaching tobacco as the leading cause of preventable death. For the two-thirds of U.S. adults who are overweight or obese, "too much" consumption means that we eat so much that our health is threatened.

Beyond our own physical well being, we also can be said to consume too much for our own financial and psychological well being. People consume and buy products for many reasons: status, entertainment, to attain happiness. To earn the money to continue consuming, people continue to work. But the more people work, the less leisure time they have to do the things that make them happy. Not finding happiness in leisure activities, people turn to shopping for happiness. This "cycle of work and spend" is, according to economist Juliet Shor, a recipe for unending misery.[8] In 2003, for example, 1.6 million households filed for bankruptcy. Average household debt in the United States in 2003, not counting mortgage debt, was more than $14,000. More than 40% of American households report that each year they spend more than they earn. In the 1980s, Americans saved almost 8% of their personal income; in 2000, the savings rate had dropped to less than 2%. The financial and psychological costs of these present consumption patterns are staggering.

But there can be moral costs to the individual consumer as well as the psychological, financial, and health costs. Moral virtues such as moderation, frugality, thriftiness, and prudence are lost in a world of consumerism and replaced by the personal vices of self-indulgence, greed, materialism. A good test of the morality of consumerism is to ask oneself: What kind of person do I want my children to become? Will they have a greater chance to be truly happy by practicing moderation and frugality, or self-indulgence and greed? In terms of our own enlightened self-interest, we consume too much.

WHY DO WE CONSUME AS WE DO?

If consumption is a problem, and if business is to have a responsibility in addressing this problem, we need to examine the causes of unsustainable consumption. If unsustainable consumption is the result simply of autonomously chosen individual desires, perhaps business has little responsibility for it. But there is good reason to think that there are other factors involved as well, factors that business can address.

Understanding consumption requires that we recognize consumption as part of a wider context of shopping, materialism, and wealth. The conventional wisdom that people consume simply to satisfy needs and considered desires collapses in the face of consumption in modern societies. Consumers in economically mature societies have long since satisfied their basic needs. People shop and buy for all sorts of reasons. One academic observer of shopping claims:

> Modern shoppers buy things to reward themselves, to satisfy psychological needs, or to make themselves feel good. Modern shoppers buy thing *because* they are expensive. They buy things to make a statement, to show off their personality, or to boost their self-esteem. Purchased items have become an affirmation of the psyche. Buy an item because you have a real physical necessity for it, in the way that our parents used to shop, has become the *least* of the modern shopper's concerns. . . . Shopping is a form of self-expression. People define themselves through their shopping. How they shop, where they shop, and what they buy serves the purpose of letting people express their desires, their needs, and their personalities.[9]

Clearly, causal explanations for shopping and consumption are many and varied. But two particular topics are relevant for evaluating the role that business plays in this. First is the long-debated issue of consumer autonomy. One explanation for why we consume as we do rests with the influence of mass marketing and advertising. Because business is responsible for influencing consumer choice, business is responsible when those choices prove problematic. The second topic concerns certain structural features of our economy. These structural features place individuals in a position in which consumption, and overconsumption, is much more rational than it otherwise would be.

Let us turn first to the topic of consumer autonomy. Conventional wisdom teaches us about consumer sovereignty and that supply is a function of demand. Critics claim that consumers are far from sovereign and in control of the marketplace. At one extreme of this debate is the claim that business, through its marketing practices, controls consumer behavior. At the other extreme is the view that business simply responds to pre-existing and independent consumer demand. Surely, both extremes are overstated. Human behavior in general is too complex a phenomenon to be controlled by marketing in any straightforward sense. But, just as unlikely is the claim that business would spend billions of dollars each year on marketing if it did not have measurable results in changed consumer behavior.

The consumer autonomy debate is complex and well developed. A full review of that debate is beyond the scope of this book. But, several points are worth mentioning. First, we should remember the description of business's purpose offered by marketing scholar Theodore Levitt. Levitt argued that "the purpose of a business is to create and keep a customer." Consumers cannot demand what does not exist and what they do not know about. Entrepreneurial business can identify consumer needs and desires even before consumers themselves can. They can also identify unmet needs and values that are not addressed in the marketplace. As the personal computer industry so clearly demonstrated, innovative products are very capable of creating their own demand. Few people in the 1970s, both among consumers and industry leaders such as IBM, could even imagine the need for a household computer. Suggesting that Apple Computer simply responded to consumer demand and had no role in creating that demand is to seriously misunderstand history.

Second, one of the most common counter-arguments to the claim that marketing can influence consumer behavior relies on the failure rates of new products. Estimates vary, but the standard claim is that a very high percentage of new products fail. If marketing can control consumer behavior, so this argument goes, heavily marketed new products would not fail at such high rates. Because they do, marketing cannot control consumer behavior. But new products failure rates also provides a counterargument to those who defend consumer sovereignty. If the consumer truly was sovereign and if business simply responds to consumer demand, then there should be few, if any, new products that fail. After all, if production responds to demand, only those products for which a market exists would be produced. A high failure rate of new products suggests that business is producing first and trying to find a market afterward. This, in turn, suggests that many businesses believe that consumer behavior can be influenced by what happens after production.

A third point is that the control of consumer behavior is a straw man. Few if any critics claim that marketing directly controls *behavior* in the sense that it can get people to do things that they do not choose to do. Rather, the claim is that marketing shapes the beliefs, desires, and expectations of consumers. Thus, consumers appear fully autonomous in that they are doing what they want. But the more precise question is whether consumer desire, not consumer behavior, is autonomous.

The concept of autonomous desire requires a more subtle analysis than autonomous behavior. As psychological afflictions such as kleptomania and addictions such as alcohol and tobacco demonstrate, not every desire that an individual has and acts upon is autonomous. We sometimes do things on the basis of a desire that is truly not our own. In *The Republic*, Plato discusses this point when he talks about being "stronger than oneself." This seemingly paradoxical statement makes sense because humans do have different types of desires. Some are simple and unreflective, more a matter of emotions and appetites. Other desires are more self-conscious, reflective, and rational. Philosophers sometimes refer to these as second-level desires because they are desires about the type of desires we have. Thus, I might want a cigarette, but not want to be a smoker. I might want to avoid exercise, but I do not want to be out of shape and lazy. I may want a hamburger and French fries, but I also do not want to eat unhealthy food and become overweight. Given that we can have conflicting wants and desires, the question is: Which should rule? Plato thought that a good person pursues rational desires, desires that are guided and controlled by a rational understanding of what is good.

Given this, it might make sense to distinguish between rational desires, irrational desires, and nonrational desires. Rational desires are those for things that are good for us; irrational desires are for things, such as tobacco or drugs, that are bad for us. Nonrational desires would be those desires that one has not rationally reflected upon and not consciously chosen. Although not actually irrational, nonrational desires are also not fully autonomous either.

Now, let us return to the short list, from page 127, of why modern consumers shop. People shop for a wide range of diverse reasons, including for entertainment, for self-esteem, for relaxation, for self-expression, to feel good, or simply on impulse. Some shopping fits the rational agent model of economics. A person has a desire, rationally examines it to determine if it will make the person happier and better off, calculates the steps required to fill that desire, performs a cost-benefit analysis to assess alternatives, and then chooses to act in a way that fulfills the desire. But much shopping for the modern consumer is nothing at all like this abstract model.

The issue is whether or not marketing can influence, create, or shape the nonrational desires of the modern consumer. Perhaps more importantly, might the constant exposure to advertising undermine the ability of consumers to do exactly the type of second-level self-reflection assumed by the rational agent model and that is necessary for autonomous desires? This point has been made by philosopher Richard Lippke, who argues that mass-marketing and persuasive advertising implicitly carry a message that undercuts the ability of consumers to rationality. In Lippke's words:

> "Ads subtly encourage the propensity to accept emotional appeals, oversimplification, superficiality, and shoddy standards of proof for claims. Evidence and arguments of the most ridiculous sorts are offered in support of advertising claims. Information about products is presented selectively (i.e., bad or questionable features are ignored), the virtues of products are exaggerated, and deception and misinformation are commonplace. The meanings of words are routinely twisted so that they are either deceptive or wholly lost."[10]

A plausible case can be made that we consume in unsustainable ways due in part to the effects of mass marketing and advertising. This is not to claim that advertising controls behavior, but that the cumulative effects of advertising and a culture of mass marketing does profoundly affect what, how, when, and why we consume what we do.

A second aspect of the explanation of contemporary consumer culture shifts the focus away from the decisions of individuals and looks instead to certain structural features of the society and economy. By "structural feature," I mean those social arrangements, expectations, and norms that provide a context in which individual decisions get made. Our individual choices are shaped to a large degree by how society is arranged. We can only choose from available options, and the options available to consumers are greatly shaped by business and economics. Certain structural features of the present business and economic context can make a choice that is individually rational but results in a socially irrational outcome.

In her analysis of why we consume, economist Juliet Shor argues that there are three important structural features of the modern economy that encourage consumers to consume in unsustainable ways.[11] First, Shor points to a "cycle of work and spend" that encourages most individuals to continue working and spending beyond the level that, in some deeper sense, they would prefer. Second, Shor argues that there is a strong "ecological bias" within the economy that discounts the true ecological costs of consumerism. Finally, Shor points to various social meanings given to consumption, particularly "consumption competitions." Each of these structural features encourage individuals to make decisions that lead to overconsumption and its attendant environmental, economic, and ethical difficulties.

The conventional wisdom concerning work suggests that market forces tend toward an equilibrium in which individuals balance their desires for income-producing work and leisure. But, present work structures prevent individuals from cutting back work to attain their leisure goals. Such benefits as health insurance, pension, and career mobility and promotion typically are not available to part-time workers. Employers have strong incentives, from tax incentives to the costs of employee benefits, to encourage present workers to work longer hours rather than hiring additional workers. These structural features make it "rational" for individuals to worker longer hours than they would prefer, which means that workers have less time to enjoy non-work leisure activities. Furthermore, because they are working longer hours and, therefore, making more money, but have less time available for leisure, greater and greater consumption becomes one of the few ways open for individuals to find rewards for their overworked life. Thus, as stated earlier, structural features of the workplace create a cycle of work and spend, a cycle that leads to overconsumption.

The second structure feature that Shor describes is a familiar theme in environmental economics. Ecological resources, from air and water to fisheries, and from the absorbent capacity of the atmosphere to CO_2-reducing capability of forests, are treated as free goods by the conventional economic wisdom. This not only leads to an over-consumption of these goods and to an overconsumption of environmentally damaging products, but it also leads to overconsumption in general. Because we are not paying the full costs of the consumption of ecological resources, it becomes easier to consume more of them than we should.

Finally, Shor points to the social meanings of consumption as a major factor in explaining why we consume as we do. Social scientists from Thorstein Veblin to the present have described the many roles that consumption plays in establishing our self-image and our social status and identity. In many ways, we are what we own. We shop and buy for entertainment, for therapy, for self-esteem, for status. We have expectations that tell us we can have it all, and we deserve it now. Our mailboxes are flooded with offers for credit cards, and retailers offer everyone, including those with bad credit history, easy credit. In a context in which positive social meanings are attached to consumption, an ordinarily rational individual is led to act in irrational ways by consuming more than is reasonable.

BUSINESS'S RESPONSIBILITY FOR CONSUMPTION

What is, and should be, the role of business in all of this? Perhaps most importantly and most directly, businesses ought to produce sustainable goods and services. If consumers overconsume on environmental, social justice, and self-interested grounds, sustainable products must diminish these harmful consequences. Two topics examined in the previous chapter suggest directions in which business might develop.

First, business can contribute to a more sustainable consumerism by shifting from a products and material-based production model to a service-based model. Business has an opportunity to discover that consumers may well "really want" services rather than more stuff. Second, improved quality of the goods and services produced can also contribute to overall sustainability. More and bigger are not always better either for consumers themselves, for society, or for business. Better quality goods—healthier, longer-lasting, more meaningful and valuable, more equitably and fairly produced—have an important contribution to make for all three pillars of sustainable societies.

But there are also responsibilities on the marketing side as well as on the production side. How would a business committed to sustainability market its products? How would a sustainable business respond to the structural features, particularly the social meaning of consumption and the cycle of work and spend that encourage unsustainable consumption?

Initially, we can say that business has a responsibility to market products with truthful and informative advertising. The truth is that consumers do have nonrational and irrational desires, and business has a choice to make in light of this fact. Marketing ought not seek to exploit or target the nonrational and irrational desires of consumers. Business ought to address the rational side of consumer demand by providing truthful and intelligible information.

Business also has responsibilities derived from the social meaning of consumption. Consumers often buy products for their social meaning, a meaning in part created and encouraged by marketing. Again, contemporary marketing is faced with a choice of what meaning gets conveyed by their marketing campaigns. Let us return to the quote from Theodore Levitt. "The purpose of business is to create and keep a customer." How can business create customers? Two well-known examples can help us understand this claim: GM's marketing of a wide range of automobiles in the mid-twentieth century, and the marketing of home computers in the late twentieth century.

If Henry Ford introduced principles of mass production to the automobile industry, it was Alfred Sloan's GM that introduced the industry to mass marketing. Although Henry Ford famously held that customers could get any color car that they wanted, as long as it was black, GM recognized the social meaning of automobile ownership. GM cars were stylish, showy, and had lots of frills. Where the early Fords were boxy, black, inexpensive, utilitarian, GM cars were designed to make a social statement. They were sleek, colorful, with lots of chrome and fins. Sloan shifted corporate leadership from the engineering department to the design department.

Under Sloan and his design chief Harley Earl, each GM division targeted a specific marketing niche, a niche that GM itself through its advertising and marketing, helped to create. Chevrolets were entry-level cars, targeting young families and blue-collar workers. Pontiacs were identified as sportier cars for more successful owners with perhaps a bit more pizzazz and style. Oldsmobiles were targeted for more conservative, white-collar workers. Buicks were owned by more successful and established professionals. And, Cadillac was for the top-level executive. If you drove a Cadillac, you had made it to the top. Perhaps most importantly, every car underwent continual updating and redesign. A new model was created every year so that owners were judged not only by the automobiles brand name but also by its year and model.

Obviously, there were problems with this approach—problems from which GM continues to suffer. Changing models every year meant that GM's marketing was, at least implicitly, criticizing its own models as inadequate only a few short months after introducing them as the latest stylist designs. More importantly, this approach meant that GM's engineering division did not keep pace with competitors in the industry. By the late 1970s, GM was losing significant business to more functional, less expensive, and better engineered cars such as the VW Beetle, Hondas, and Toyotas. Interestingly enough, each of these brands also emphasized the social meaning of the automobile. Driving a VW Beetle in the 1960s and 1970s, for example, made a clear social and political statement.

The lesson from GM is that markets can be created and controlled by business. To the degree that consumption has social meaning, consumer demand is not, by definition, a result of individual choice. Consumer demand generated out of social meaning is not a given to which business responds. It is a dynamic phenomenon that is and can be shaped by marketing. Most importantly, if marketing can be held partially liable for bad consumption, it can also hold the key for creating better, more sustainable consumption as well.

As a second example, consider the creation of the home computing market that exploded in the 1980s and 1990s. As a student in the 1970s, I typed papers on a Smith-Corona manual typewriter. As a young faculty member in the 1980s, I graduated to an IBM electric. At that time, I could not even imagine what I would do with a computer, let alone think I could ever afford one. If Apple Computer and IBM had waited for consumer demand to direct their business, we would all still be typing on electric typewriters, paying bills by mail, and standing in lines in stores and libraries. There simply was no demand for computers, software, MP3 players, video games, online banking, virus protection software, search engines, and cable modems in 1980. By 2000, these and other high-tech products and services were driving an unprecedented economic boom.

I suggest that we may be standing at a similar threshold. Consumers are not demanding more sustainable products and services because, like the consumers facing the computer revolution in 1980, most people have no idea what such a world would look like and what they will need to flourish in a sustainable future. Creative businesses and entrepreneurial individuals will not wait for consumer demand to magically appear. Sustainable products, supported by creative and imaginative marketing, can create their own demand if business is daring enough to try. The social meaning of consumerism is the product of social forces, including commercial marketing and advertising. There is no reason to believe that this meaning cannot be shifted toward a more sustainable consumer lifestyle.

I would like to turn to a second of the structural features of consumerism described by Juliet Shor. Shor tells us that a cycle of work and spend is an important factor in explaining modern overconsumption. Many people in consumerist societies find themselves working longer and longer hours. One result is that they have more money to spend, but less time in which to spend it. In part because of longer work hours, people feel that they deserve extra, and spend the added income on more and more frills. Frills that, perhaps, they do not "really want and value" but which serve as substitutes for other values. The major alternative to this work and spend cycle is to work and spend less. But this option is often unavailable, not the least because only full-time jobs carry health and insurance benefits that would be unaffordable on part-time salaries.

Businesses have opportunities to change the structure of our working as well as our consuming lives. Health and other benefits for part-time workers, flexible benefit packages in which workers can trade-off pay and other benefits for more leisure time, and job-sharing opportunities can help workers escape cycle of work and spend. Sabbatical leaves of the type common in higher education can be a means for employees to strike a more reasonable balance between work and family. Such sabbatical leaves can also help create healthier and more productive employees.

PHILOSOPHICAL REFLECTIONS ON CONSUMERISM

As we reflect on the present economic and environmental challenges and consider our responsibilities to create a sustainable future, it is easy to think that we are facing ethical issues that are unprecedented in human history. The scope of these challenges may well be unprecedented, but the ethical and philosophical questions that they raise are not. It can be instructive to step back from the immediacy of our present concerns and reflect for a moment on how similar issues have been examined by others.

Early in Book II of *The Republic*, Plato begins the formation of the just city with a discussion of topics not unlike the ones we have just examined. "Come then," says Socrates to Adeimantus, "let us create a city from the beginning. And it is our needs, it seems, that will create it. Surely our first and greatest need is to provide food to sustain life." Shelter and clothing are identified next as the second and third needs before Socrates shifts to the question of production. "How will the city adequately provide for all this? Should one man be a farmer, another a builder, and another a weaver? Or should we add a cobbler and some other craftsmen to look after our physical needs?" (369d)

Here, early in *The Republic*, we have Plato raising two significant philosophical questions about economics: by what criteria should we decide what gets produced, and what are the socially best means for production? Plato's initial answer to the first question is given in terms of satisfying needs. His answer to the second question is given in terms of a division of labor according to ability. The socialist dictum "from each according to ability, to each according to need" finds its first expression here early in Plato's *The Republic*.

But Socrates is forced to soon revise this initial description of a just society in the face of criticism offered by the very dissatisfied Glaucon. "You make these men have their feast without relish" and have created "city of pigs," says Glaucon. Clearly, according to Glaucon, the happier and more conventional life is a more luxurious life that satisfies wider desires than mere needs. For his part, Socrates believes that the simple city already described is the good and healthy city. Reluctantly, he admits that it probably will not satisfy many and agrees to consider the more "luxurious" city. Describing this luxurious city as "feverish," Socrates acknowledges that it is the more likely that issues of justice and injustice will arise in this new expanded city. "The city must be made bigger again. This healthy one isn't adequate any more, but must already be gorged with a bulky mass of things which are not in the cities because of need."

Increasing consumer demand and economic growth leads to the creation of a growing, and unhealthy, city. To satisfy this growing demand, all sorts of new jobs and consumer goods must be created. More food, and less healthy food, will be demanded. As a result, there will be a "much greater need of doctors if we follow this way of life rather than the earlier one." Finally, there will be the need for a military class, because "the land, which was sufficient for feeding the people who were there will now be too small." In this fact, Socrates uncovered the origins of war. Insatiable consumer demand and accompanying economic growth lead to the need to take "our neighbor's land if we are to have sufficient for pasture and agriculture, and they in turn will seek to take ours." This happens to men who "let themselves go to the unlimited acquisition of money, and overstep the bounds of what is necessary." (*The Republic*, 372–374)

Plato's story is a familiar one. In the nineteenth and early twentieth centuries, economists confronted a similar paradox. For the first time in modern history, industrialization and economic development had produced economies in which basic needs were being fulfilled. The progress represented by technological and economic growth promised a world in which the basic needs of every person could be met.

A conventional economic assumption at the time was that people worked to satisfy their needs. The implication of this assumption was that once those needs were satisfied, people would begin to work less. But, less work would result in lower overall demand—because less would be produced and people would have less to spend—and this lowered demand would in turn result in an economic downturn or recession. Thus, the success of an economic system would seem to contain within itself the seeds of its own destruction. Of course, nothing of the sort happened for reasons that Plato would have understood. People have an insatiable desire for "relish" in their lives and are soon dissatisfied with what they have.

One can also consider parallels with Plato's luxurious city and contemporary consumerist culture. Insatiable desires and luxurious foods do require that we need more doctors than we otherwise would. Preventable deaths related to heart disease, tobacco, and obesity have obvious parallels. War, fueled by the requirements of oil-driven modern economies, seems to have parallels as well.

Plato, of course, thought that justice was still possible in such a city, but it would be tenuous. Three major conditions, each of which Plato admits is radical and unlikely to occur in fourth century B.C. Athens, must come about for such a society to become and remain just: women must be treated as equals and given equal educational opportunities; private possessions, including spouses and children, must be abolished and replaced with communal ownership; and, famously, philosophers must become kings, or those who rule must learn to philosophize.

The role of the philosopher king in Plato's city is to moderate and temper the insatiable desires of the people. The parallel role for reason within the individual soul is to moderate and direct our own appetites. The moderating principle for both cities and individuals is knowledge of the good. Our consumer desires are as natural as any other part of human nature, but *what* is desired will spell the difference between a healthy and just life and an unhealthy and unjust one. Perhaps the parallels are too few and we should not draw any conclusions from Plato's story. But justice does seem tenuous in a consumerist society.

Plato also offered an analysis of the relation between our desires and human happiness that remains especially relevant to a contemporary discussion of consumerism. One common understanding of human happiness, as common in Plato's time as it is among contemporary economists, is that people are happy when they get what they desire. But this immediately raises a major philosophical and ethical difficulty. At least at times, it would seem that conforming to ethical rules and fulfilling our ethical duties run counter to what we desire. Thus, it would seem that being ethical will not always make us happy, and pursuing happiness may run counter to ethics. Thus arises the long-standing belief that happiness and self-interest conflict with ethics.

One alternative, perhaps best exemplified in the ethical system of the philosopher Immanuel Kant, is to accept this tension and insist that the moral imperative obligates us even when it conflicts with our desires and happiness. But Plato's solution rejected the essential conflict between desire and ethics. If we are happy when we get what we desire, and if some of our desires are for unethical things, then we should change our desires rather than forsaking happiness. If we desire what is good, then we can be both happy and just, and we can become happy by doing the ethically good thing.

It is not uncommon for discussions of consumerism to sound more akin to Kant than to Plato. Many would argue that the conspicuous consumption associated with commercial culture should be abandoned, despite the enjoyment that it provides, in favor of a more frugal and sensible lifestyle. One often gets the idea that sustainable societies can offer only a dour and cheerless lifestyle. But, the lesson from Plato is that we can have it both ways. We can both be happy and do the right thing. We can learn to desire the good, and sustainable, lifestyle. We can enjoy food, but should desire good food rather than junk food. We can still desire fine clothing and fine homes, but should develop the informed and cultured tastes of the finer things. More stuff is not better, it is only more. The desire for better things, not more things, is best. Rational desires alone offer the possibility for both happiness and an ethical future.

Endnotes

1 See Report of the Oslo Symposium on Sustainable Consumption, January 1994, Ministry of Environment, Oslo, Norway.

2 The Lowell Center

3 The first estimate is from Juliet Shor, "Why Do We Consume So Much?" in *Contemporary Issues in Business Ethics, 5e*, Joseph DesJardins and John McCall, eds., (Belmont, CA: Wadsworth Publishing, 2005), pp. 373–379. The second estimate is from C.K. Prahalad, *The Fortune at the Bottom of the Pyramid*, (Upper Saddle River, NJ: Wharton Publishing, 2005), p. 3.

4 *State of the World 2004*, Worldwatch Institute, Washington, D.C.

5 Household size is taken from U.S. Census Bureau, www.census.gov/population/ www/socdemo/hh-fam.html. Home size is from Shor, op. cit., p. 373.

6 Juliet Shor, "Why Do We Consume So Much?", delivered as the Clemens Lecture at St. John's University, published in *Contemporary Issues in Business Ethics* Joseph DesJardins and John McCall, eds., (Belmont, CA, Wadsworth Publishing, 2005).

7 I take this distinction between what economic activities do for us and to us, from the U.S. Catholic Bishop's pastoral letter on the American economy, *Economic Justice for All* (National Catholic Conference, Washington, D.C., 1986).

8 Shor in DesJardins and McCall, p. 375.

9 *"Why We Shop: Emotional Rewards and Retail Strategies"* by Jim Pooler (Praeger Publishing, Westport, CT), 2003. pp. 1–3.

10 Richard Lippke, *Radical Business Ethics* (Lanham, MD: Rowman and Littlefield, 1995), pp. 108–109.

11 Shor in DesJardins and McCall, p. 375.

chapter nine

Creating Sustainable Professions and Communities

INTRODUCTION

The topics discussed in the previous two chapters, production and consumption, have received considerable attention within the sustainability literature. This is not surprising because these topics are central to business and economic thinking. Given the framework of the $I = PAT$ formula, consumption and production are at the heart of environmental concerns as well. But the overlap of economics, the environment, and ethics has implications for other aspects of business that have just begun to receive more attention within the sustainability literature. In this chapter, two areas that are likely to impact the future of sustainable business are explored: the development of the functional areas of business in a sustainable future, and the role of business in the evolution of sustainable communities.

The previous chapters have implicitly assumed a managerial point of view. The business audiences for those chapters were the managers and executives charged with making policy decisions for business. But this managerial perspective does not exhaust the areas in which individuals pursue business careers. Many students contemplating business careers are interested in functional areas outside of management *per se*: marketing, accounting, finance, human resources, operations. Students and professionals with these skills and interests, whether they are employed within a corporate setting or not, have much to contribute to the sustainable economy of the future.

SUSTAINABLE MARKETING

The demand for sustainable goods and services among the billions of people living at the bottom of the economic pyramid represents what is perhaps the greatest marketing opportunity in history. Billions of human beings have tremendous unmet needs. Although charity and corporate philanthropy

certainly have roles to play in addressing these needs, such approaches will
ultimately prove unsustainable. The world needs an approach to poverty
that helps the poor create a sustainable social and economic system through
which they can achieve long-term prosperity.

C.K. Prahalad has made a convincing case that such an approach is both
practically attainable and ethically and economically legitimate. Prahalad
argues that

> If we stop thinking of the poor as victims or as a burden and start recognizing
> them as resilient and creative entrepreneurs and value-conscious consumers, a
> whole new world of opportunity will open up. Four billion poor can be the
> engine of the next round of global trade and prosperity. . . . What is needed is a
> better approach to help the poor, an approach that involves partnering with
> them to innovate and achieve sustainable win-win scenarios where the poor
> are actively engaged and, at the same time, the companies providing products
> and services to them are profitable."[1]

Accomplishing such goals will require a significant revision to the standard marketing paradigm. Business must, in Prahalad's phrase, "create the
capacity to consume" among the world's poor. Creating this capacity is
exactly the challenge for sustainable marketing.

Creating the capacity to consume among the world's poor will require a
transformation in the conceptual framework of global marketing. Part of this
will require marketers to overcome their own mistaken assumptions about
the world's poor. Prahalad points out that the world's poor do have significant purchasing power, albeit in the aggregate rather than on a per capita
basis. They can also be technologically sophisticated, brand-conscious, and
value-conscious. But marketing to the world's poor will also require some
creative steps from business. Prahalad mentions three principles as key to
marketing to the poor: affordability, access, availability.

The market potential at the base of the pyramid lies in the aggregate and
not in per capita spending. One crucial element of marketing to the poor will
be to make goods and services affordable on a per capita basis. As an example, Prahalad points out that the shampoo market in India is equal, in gross
amount of shampoo sales, to the shampoo market in the United States, but to
market shampoo in India, firms will need to make their products available in
smaller and more affordable sizes. Single-serve sizes for such commodities as
shampoo, ketchup, coffee, medicines, soaps, tea, and spices have already
proved to be very successful marketing tools in India.

Given longer and more erratic work hours and a lack of personal transportation, the poor often lack access to markets. Creative marketing can find
ways to provide easier access to their products. Longer store hours, wider
and more convenient distribution channels can reach consumers otherwise
left out of the market. So, too, can imaginative financing, credit, and pricing
schemes. Finally, innovative marketing can ensure that products are available

where and when the world's poor need them. Base of the pyramid consumers tend to be cash customers with incomes that are unpredictable. A distributional system that ensures product availability at the time and place when customers are ready and able to make the purchase can help create the capacity to consume.

Beyond the need for sustainable marketing among the base of the world's economic pyramid, many opportunities exist elsewhere in the global economy. More traditional marketing is also evolving in the direction of sustainability.

In what can be thought of as the first wave of environmental marketing, "Green Marketing" involved selling products to an environmentally motivated market. Beginning as early as the first Earth Day in April 1970, marketers recognized a growing consumer demand for products that were environmentally beneficial or at least environmentally benign. This first wave of environmental marketing worked to identify, target, and exploit this new movement for green products. Widespread criticisms accompanied these initiatives from the start, claiming that the alleged environmental benefits for such "green products" were at best window dressing and at worst manipulative and deceptive.

No doubt such deceptive practices will continue in the development of a sustainable economy and sustainable business. One area for future marketing research, therefore, will involve developing standards for determining what does and does not qualify as a sustainable product. "Green" or "eco" or "sustainable" of "cradle-to-cradle" labeling, for example, will likely play a role in future marketing. Just as standards for organic food products and nutrition have evolved over time, eco-labeling will surely go through a similar history. The ability to help establish best practices for sustainable labeling, as was the case for establishing standards in sustainable building design, provides the marketing profession with strong business reasons for becoming involved before regulatory standards are mandated.

It is common to find the field of marketing divided according to four variables: product, pricing, promotion, and distribution. Each of these areas provides opportunities for marketing professionals to develop sustainable practices.[2] We can sketch directions in which sustainable marketing practices might develop for each of these variables.

As the discussion in previous chapters suggests, significant progress toward sustainability will depend on the sustainability of products themselves. Discovering what the consumer "really wants" and developing the products to meet those wants have always been among the primary marketing challenges. Meeting the real needs of present and future generations within ecological constraints can be understood simply as a refinement of this traditional marketing objective.

Consider, for example, the business differences between marketing the physical pieces of computer hardware and marketing computing services. Should Dell or HP be in the business of selling computer components, or are they selling the service to provide consumers with up-to-date computing processing, software, data storage? The marketing department should be at the forefront of identifying the real needs of consumers so that a business can develop the long-term relationships with consumers that will ensure both financial and ecological sustainability.

Another aspect of marketing involves the design and creation of products. William McDonough has often described environmental regulation as a design problem; a product or production process that pollutes and wastes resources is a poorly designed product or process. Regulatory mandates usually result when business has a poorly designed product or process. Marketing departments should also be involved in the design of products, finding ways to build sustainability into the very design of each product.

Finally, marketing professionals have an opportunity to influence the packaging of products. Overpackaging and the use of petroleum-based plastics are packaging issues already under environmental scrutiny. Imagine the marketing opportunities if a major soft-drink bottler such as Coke or Pepsi turned to corn-based biodegradable plastics for their bottles. Imagine what the marketing department of major mail-order companies such as Land's End or L.L. Bean could do if their catalogues were printed on recycled paper. Imagine the marketing opportunities, and responsibilities, of a company such as Procter & Gamble moving toward recycled cardboard for its packaging.

These three areas come together clearly within the context of extended producer responsibility and take-back legislation. These regulatory developments will be seen as burdens and as barriers to profit by some firms. But more creative firms will see opportunities here for generating entire new markets. Take-back legislation provides strong incentives for re-designing products in ways that make it easier to reuse and recycle. Marketing services rather than products, of course, will be the most efficient means for accomplishing this.

A second aspect of marketing is price. On several occasions in this book, we considered claims that the environmental costs of resources, the "natural capital" on which most firms rely, are not factored into the price of most products. Marketing professionals should play a role in setting prices that reflect a product's true ecological cost.

At first glance, this might seem a peculiar area in which to expect business to move. Internalizing environmental externalities sounds like a polite way of suggesting that business ought to raise its prices. Such a strategy would seem, at best, unrealistic. Government regulation is more likely to move business in this direction than voluntary action. Without government mandate across the board of an industry, to internalize the costs of natural capitalism into one's products will put a company at a comparative disadvantage.

On the other hand, setting prices in such a way that more sustainable products are priced competitively with other products is a more reasonable strategy for sustainable marketing. Ordinarily, we might think that pricing is a straightforward and objective process. One starts with the costs of producing a product, adds a reasonable rate of return, and the result is asking price. Ultimately, the actual price is whatever buyer and seller agree upon. However, this simple model misses some important complexities. To understand some of the complexities of price, and the role of marketing in this, consider the example of hybrid automobiles.

Like any new product, a hybrid automobile required investments in research, design, production, and marketing long before it could be brought to market. For such a complex product as a hybrid automobile, these investments were substantial, well into the hundreds of millions of dollars for each automaker who produces a hybrid. Setting a price for this product involves a complicated process of projecting sales, markets, and a product's life cycle. In one sense, the very first hybrid cost millions of dollars to manufacture, well beyond an affordable and marketable price. Businesses normally takes a loss on a new product until such time as economies of scale kick in to lower costs and market share develops sufficiently to produce a revenue stream that can begin to pay down the initial investment and generate profits. Marketing professionals who are aware of sustainability concerns have much to contribute in establishing prices that protect sustainable products from short-term cost-benefit analyses.

Consider also how price functions with such business practices as sales, manufacturer's rebates, cash-back incentives to consumers, bonuses to sales staff, and the use of loss leaders in retailing. Obviously, price is often manipulated for many marketing reasons, including promotion to help gain a foothold in a market. Short-term losses are often justified in pricing decisions by appeal to long-term considerations. This seems a perfect fit for sustainable marketing goals.

Perhaps nowhere is price a more crucial element of marketing than it is in marketing to the base of the economic pyramid. Small profit margins and efficient distribution systems within large markets, as demonstrated so clearly by such large retailers as Wal-Mart, can prove to be a highly successful business model. An ethically praiseworthy goal would be to export this marketing ingenuity to serve the cause of global sustainability.

A third aspect of marketing, of course, is the promotion and advertising of products. Marketers clearly have many opportunities and responsibilities for promoting sustainable products. Already there are developing markets for environmentally sustainable products. As in any marketing context, identifying and reaching those markets will be an important task for sustainable marketing. A marketing department should be at the forefront of identifying and targeting consumers who are already inclined to buy sustainable products.

Marketing also has a responsibility to help shape consumer demand, encouraging consumers to demand more sustainable products from business. Without question, marketing has already shown how powerful a force it can be in shaping consumer demand. Marketing has played a major role in creating various social meanings for shopping and buying. Sustainable marketing can help create the social meanings and consumer expectations supportive of sustainable goals. An often overlooked aspect of advertising is its educational function. Consumers learn from advertising, and marketers have a responsibility as educators. Helping consumers learn the value of sustainable products, helping them become sustainable consumers, is an important role for sustainable marketing.

Certainly one aspect of product promotion will involve the "green labeling" described previously. Just as ingredient labels, nutrition labels, and warning labels have become normal and standardized, environmental pressure may well create a public demand for environmental and sustainable labeling.

The final aspect of marketing involves the channels of distribution that move a product from producer to consumer. Patrick Murphy suggests two directions in which marketing can develop sustainable channels.[3] As typically understood, marketing channels involve such things as transportation, distribution, inventory, and the like. Recent advances in marketing have emphasized just in time inventory control, large distribution centers, and sophisticated transportation schemes. Murphy foresees new sustainability options being added to this model that emphasize fuel efficiency and alternative fuel technologies used in transportation, more localized and efficient distribution channels, and a greater reliance on electronic rather than physical distribution. More efficient distribution channels can also serve under-served base of the pyramid consumers as well.

Consider, as an example, how the publishing industry has evolved its channels of distribution. Originally, books, magazines, catalogs, or newspapers were printed in one location and then distributed via truck, rail, or air across the country. More modern practices piloted by such companies as *USA Today* and the *Wall Street Journal* send electronic versions of the content to localized printers who publish and distribute the final product locally. Textbook publishers do a similar thing when they allow users to select specific content and create a custom-published book for each use. As subscriptions to hardcopy publications decline, many newspapers, magazines, and catalogues are taking this a step further by moving toward on-line publishing.

Murphy also describes a second aspect of the channel variable in marketing that promises significant sustainability rewards. "Reverse channels" refers to the growing marketing practice of taking back one's products after their useful life. The life cycle responsibility and "take-back" models described in previous chapters will likely fall to marketing departments. The same department that is responsible for sending a product out into the marketplace should expect the responsibility for finding ways to take back that product to dispose, recycle, or reuse it.[4]

SUSTAINABLE ACCOUNTING, AUDITING, FINANCE

It is an old adage of management that "one can't manage what one can't measure." One of the greatest challenges awaiting the functional business areas of accounting, auditing, and finance is the creation and refinement of sustainability measures and reports. Virtually every area of managerial responsibility for sustainability initiatives will require accountants, auditors, and the financial service sector to develop assessment and measurement tools to guide decision-making. Environmental audits, "triple bottom line" accounting, and corporate sustainability reports already exist, suggesting that, in the future, accountants and auditors will be asked to examine corporate sustainability.

Managerial accounting and auditing has much to contribute to the development of internal sustainability audits. The emergence of the corporate social responsibility movement in recent decades has advanced the evolution of internal audit reports from those involving only financial considerations to broader social audits. A business committed to sustainability will need people to determine what that means, how it can be measured, and to track progress in this direction. Sustainability audits would do exactly this.

For example, the international accounting and consulting firm of KMPG conducts an international survey of corporate sustainability reports. According to KPMG:

> Since the publication of KPMG's International Survey of Environmental Reporting in 1999, there has been significant change in the number, scope and quality of reports produced by companies. The KPMG 2002 International Survey on Corporate Sustainability Reporting shows that reporting is now becoming mainstream for big corporations, with 45 percent of Global Fortune Top 250 companies now publishing a report. The focus of these reports is slowly shifting from the inclusion of only environmental performance to combined environmental, social and economic reports (i.e., sustainability reports), and an increasing number of reports are being externally verified.[5]

Independent accountants and auditors can also expect the evolution of their own fields to include sustainability measures. As KMPG suggests, external verification of sustainability reports is growing, and professionals working for public accounting firms have a role to play both in developing external standards and in attesting to corporate progress toward sustainability. Many other external agencies and NGOs such as the United Nations Environment Programme (UNEP) are working to develop sustainability measures, encourage their adoption by business, and to monitor corporate sustainability progress.

A number of interesting sustainability questions face finance, both within corporate setting and as an industry itself. Herman Daly reminds us that prudent capital investment within a firm is directed at the limiting factor on production: if we have parts, labor, facilities, but few customers, we invest in marketing; if we have customers, parts and facilities, but few workers, we invest in hiring, etc. When natural capital becomes the limiting factor, prudent investment must be directed toward natural resources.

Within the financial industry itself, Socially Responsible Investment (SRI) already represents a growing field. There is much work still to be done in developing criteria and measures for identifying and assessing socially responsible investments. But one growing aspect of SRI in general is the interest in investing in firms committed to sustainability. For example, in 1999 Dow Jones launched a group of sustainability indexes to track the financial performance of businesses committed to sustainability goals. The Dow Jones Sustainability Index also helps asset managers develop standards and benchmarks for measuring and tracking their portfolios of sustainable businesses.

We need to see sustainability programs outlined for the banking and insurance industries. In general, both banking and insurance function to help customers manage risks, and, therefore, developing practices that manage the financial risks associated with unsustainable systems and actions is a natural evolution for these fields. The insurance industry is already playing a role in debates about global warning as insurance rates rise in low-lying coastal regions most affected by rising sea levels and increasingly severe weather patterns. Banks also will have a role to play in creating and managing financing for such policies as trading pollution credits, especially if international trading schemes are developed as a result of the Kyoto Protocol on CO_2 emissions.[6]

Also, as described previously, microfinance and microcredit policies piloted by such institutions as the Grameen Bank of Bangladesh can make tremendous contributions to the development of sustainable industries in the poorest regions in both developed and less developed countries. Mainstream banks have shied away from micro-lending, but this is an area that creative and responsible bankers ought to pursue. The success of the Grameen Bank shows that this is yet another sustainable practice that involves both ethical responsibilities and economic opportunities.

Some evidence suggests that a necessary component for successful micro-lending programs is the initial creating of micro-savings program.[7] Both the Grameen Bank and the Bank of Madura in India have created innovative programs in which local community leaders helped organize and administer small and locally managed banking programs. These programs began by building trust among community members, educating them about the benefits and responsibilities of savings, and eventually transforming a local micro-saving system into a local micro-lending system.

SUSTAINABLE HR AND OPERATIONS

Two other functional areas in business deserve mention as important resources in the movement toward sustainability. Human Resource (HR) departments oversee working conditions of employees, and operations managers oversee day-to-day operation of plants and facilities. Both areas have a role to play in a sustainable business.

There are two areas in which HR officials can make particular contributions. HR officers will be challenged to create sustainable, healthy, and safe workplaces. Because workers, rather than consumers, typically face the greatest risks with toxic products, HR professionals should become advocates for eliminating toxic components and ingredients in products. Furthermore, just as local HR departments have been drawn into debates about sweatshops and other inadequate working conditions throughout a company's entire supply chain, one can expect a similar development concerning worker exposure to toxic products throughout the entire supply chain and distribution channels of production.

A second area in which HR departments can contribute would involve steps to alleviate the cycle of work and spend and overconsumption that contributes to unsustainable lifestyles. As mentioned in Chapter Eight, creative HR departments could develop flexible work schedules and benefit packages that would help employees step back from the work and spend cycle and bring some balance and needed leisure to their lives. Economist Juliet Shor has argued that overconsumption is fueled by a cycle of work and spend; people spend more as an antidote and reward for working more, and then must work even more to pay for increased spending. This cycle, in turn, is fueled by workplace expectations, demands for overtime work, and needed health insurance benefit packages for which part-time workers are not qualified. To the degree that overconsumption can be countered by a better balance of work and leisure, HR officers have an opportunity to help create this more stable lifestyle. Creative HR departments could also encourage job-sharing, flexible benefit packages, and other programs to relieve workplace stress and encourage a less consumerist lifestyle.

Many companies already promote healthy living and wellness practices in the workplace. HR departments regularly promote programs that discourage smoking, encourage exercise, and provide cancer screening, mammograms, blood pressure testing, and other health care services to employees. Some companies are also including workshops on voluntary simplicity and other anti-consumerism programs as part of their wellness-at-work programming.[8]

The operations side of business may well play a role in the movement toward sustainability that is equal to any other business role. In what is sometimes considered an unglamorous side of business, operations managers and engineers have day-to-day oversight responsibility for much of business practice. Operations typically are understood to include such departments as purchasing or procurement, facilities management, and inventory management. Each of these arenas can make direct contributions to sustainable business practice.

As described previously, a sustainable business will require changes throughout its entire supply chain, and this responsibility will fall to those managers charged with purchasing and procurement decisions. When sustainable products already exist in the supply chain, purchasing agents have an opportunity to shift business to those suppliers with sustainable products. We have already discussed such situations with examples of corn-based plastics and recycled paper. But such a change will not be without challenge. Loyalty to, and confidence in, long-term suppliers will work against any shift to new sustainable supply markets. But inertia can also explain a reluctance to use the purchasing power of business to support sustainable new products. When sustainable products do not exist in a supply chain, purchasing departments have an opportunity to use their market power to demand such products. One area in which purchasing departments could make a significant contribution in this respect would be to encourage or demand that suppliers provide take-back services.

Facilities managers can have responsibility for such diverse areas as heating and air conditions systems, lighting, furnishings and supplies, maintenance and custodial services, waste and trash management, telecommunications, and computing services. Obviously, energy use within a business will be a major way that firms can move toward sustainability. Sustainable facilities management could start with such simple decisions as compact fluorescent lighting, motion detectors to conserve, and energy efficient systems for heating an air conditioning. Creating a market for and using stationary fuel cells for energy generation and back-up would be a more creative contribution to energy use. The department responsible for waste management could easily create incentives and programs for recycling and waste reduction and elimination.

The design and construction of facilities themselves is an important side of creating a sustainable business. Working with architects and builders to attain Leadership in Energy and Environmental Design (LEED) certification of building projects would be a standard within the profession. Even when short-term costs are higher, the evidence overwhelmingly supports the fact that investment in sustainable design and construction will produce long-term economic benefits. The redesign of Ford Motor Company's Rouge River plant by William McDonough stands as a symbol of what can be done when facilities are managed for sustainability.

McDonough's company has also promoted the use of "green roofs," the practice of using grasses and plants as roofing materials. Instead of relying on asphalt, metal, or wood shingles, this process covers the roof with soil and plants. Such a roof not only is longer lasting, but it absorbs rain and storm water, provides a sound-barrier, creates oxygen, and provides habitat for other living species. The Gap's corporate headquarters in San Bruno, California, as well as Ford's Rouge River plant employ green roofing. McDonough estimates that Ford has saved millions of dollars in storm-water equipment as a result.

Facilities managers also have many opportunities in managing the grounds and landscape surrounding a business. Minimizing asphalt parking lots, substituting gravel or even grass, controls run-off from storms by providing a natural means to absorb and filter rainwater. Planting native species of grasses and plants not only saves money for mowing and maintenance, but reduces the need for irrigation and fertilizer and pesticide use.

SUSTAINABLE COMMUNITIES

The final future direction I want to mention concerns the communities in which business operates. Like many other aspects of sustainability, the development of sustainable communities provides business with both risks and opportunities. Consider how businesses were affected by community planning in the twentieth century. Road construction and the expansion of public utilities and other infrastructure into the suburbs provided the occasion for sprawl and urban decay. Businesses that had been located within urban centers, from manufacturing to retail, fought to survive; most moved to follow the population or went out of business. Their move out of cities, of course, created a cycle of sprawl as employees and customers followed. Small indigenous and local firms, often located within walking distance from residential neighborhoods, had to compete with international businesses and "Big Box" retailers for both customers and workers. The construction and real estate industries, the automotive industry, and large retail industries thrived in the last half of the twentieth century with the growth of sprawling suburbs.

There are good reasons for thinking that this ever-expanding model of community development is coming to an end. Developed societies will need to find ways to build healthier and more livable communities than the ones characterized by sprawl. Inevitably, some industries will benefit from these changes, some will not. In the sustainable future, we will see a growing expectation that business should play a role in the development of sustainable communities.

Conventional wisdom tends to downplay the relationship between business and its local community or, perhaps more precisely, thinks of the local community solely in terms of a collection of actual and potential customers. But, in fact, there is a very dynamic relationship between business, local governments, community organizations, and citizens. The relationship is clearly seen in the zoning regulations that exist in every community.

Whenever we discuss government regulation, it is easy to think solely in terms of large federal bureaucracies such as the Environmental Protection Agency (EPA), the US Food and Drug Administration (FDA), the Federal Trade Commission (FTC), and Occupational Safety and Health Association (OSHA). But every business in every location that it operates must work with building codes and zoning regulations that are created and enforced by local communities. Tax policy is another area often overlooked when government regulation is discussed. Local and state tax decisions, from taxes on labor (income tax) to property tax and sales tax, can have profound influences on business decision-making. Almost every line in federal, state, and local tax code will benefit some businesses and cost others.

Building and zoning codes regulate everything from a business's location to its design and building materials, and from the size of parking lots and sidewalks to distances from other buildings and hours of operation. Although such regulations apply to every business, they are particularly dominant in the housing, construction, and real estate industries. As often as not, local building codes and zoning regulations can be as much a hindrance to sustainable communities as a help. Building codes might include plumbing regulations that prohibit composting toilets, or electrical codes that limit the use of home fuel-cell generators, both beneficial technologies from a sustainability perspective. Zoning codes might restrict the use of wind turbines or require setbacks that prevent cluster housing units.

Communities also provide business with the infrastructure that is essential to support every business. Roads and transportation are perhaps the most obvious, but utilities such as water, sewer, and electricity are equally necessary as are fire and police protection.

Local and regional governments also set tax policy regarding income, property, and sales tax. Taxes may discourage some local businesses, and tax benefits can provide incentives to others. Many local governments use tax increment financing (TIFs) as a means to support targeted economic development. Tax-increment financing is a process by which tax revenues that are projected to be generated from economic development are used to finance that development. Essentially, a city or other governmental authority grants business the right to divert money that would have been paid in taxes to help finance new business development. Once the new development occurs, the public benefits from the ongoing increased tax revenues produced by that new development.

All of these more localized government actions encourage some businesses and create barriers to others. For the most part, local governments have not been very intentional in how these decisions are used to shape their communities. But, as local jurisdictions become more conscious about the need to create sustainable and livable communities, we can expect that all of these local governmental tools will be used to encourage economic practices that contribute to, rather than detract from, sustainability.

Consider the dynamic relationship between local zoning regulations, the development of residential neighborhoods, and the construction and real estate industries. Keep in mind that new home construction is one of the primary economic indicators and drivers of national economic performance.

Housing density is one of the major components of zoning regulations. Distances between homes and setbacks from roads and property lines are very tightly regulated in most zoning laws. In suburban residential neighborhoods, modern zoning regulations typically require significant setbacks from streets and large lot sizes, perhaps one-forth acre or more. Zoning regulations also govern the width of streets and require enough off-street parking to accommodate several cars. Apartments and other types of mixed housing are often prohibited in residential neighborhoods of single-family homes.

The result is that this kind of zoning creates strong incentives for builders to leave no open space or natural areas within a development. Because they are limited in the number of homes, they can build in any development; all the available space is used for housing and, because the density is limited, there is an incentive to build large, and more profitable, homes. Because most commercial uses, for example, grocery stores, are prohibited from such residential zones, zoning regulations encourage automobile use. Often enough, the costs of constructing sidewalks is assessed directly to homeowners creating further incentives for driving. Zoning regulations and automobile use create strong incentives for continued urban sprawl and the continued loss of open space and natural areas.

In recent years, many communities have begun to question the wisdom of this approach. Roads and infrastructure are extended out into the suburbs, whereas existing infrastructure decays in cities. New schools are built in suburbs, as older schools are abandoned in town. A movement called "smart growth" is directing communities in the direction of more sustainable community development strategies.[9]

Rather than building roads and infrastructure, or encouraging economic development of just any kind, and then stepping back to see what type of community develops, smart growth encourages the intentional design of communities. One important aspect is to design communities around the needs of people, not cars. Among the smart-growth proposals are several that will impact business.

Sustainable communities will need to reinvest and redevelop existing neighborhoods and cities. Large urban areas that were abandoned in the last decades of the twentieth century will need to be reclaimed and revitalized in the twenty-first Living in and around cities will make people less reliant on automobiles, especially for such simple tasks as travel for groceries and schools. Mass transit is more economical and a more attractive option in cities than it is in suburbs.

Smart growth also looks for ways to preserve open space, farmland, and natural areas. Mixed-housing types and mixed-land uses are other ways to build more sustainable communities. Cluster-housing developments will replace the standard "cookie-cutter" development. Cluster housing maintains the same overall density in a housing development, but clusters the homes closer together to leave significant natural areas undisturbed. These developments also lower infrastructure costs as roads, water, sewer, and utilities are more centrally located.

Where zoning and tax policies encouraged sprawl in the past, sustainable communities will use those same policy tools to encourage smart growth. TIFs can be used for the creation of eco-industrial parks and other industrial ecology designs. Already, several states have mandated that new public construction must meet LEED building standards. It is a short step from there to the incorporation of LEED standards into all zoning regulations and building codes. Business ought to be anticipating such changes, and responsible businesses ought to be helping bring them about.

Imagine for a moment what a good city and a good community would look like. If you could start from scratch and design the ideal community in which you would live, work, and raise a family, what would you choose? I think few people would imagine a world of strip malls, fast food restaurants clustered together with tacky neon lights flashing, and row upon row of uninteresting tract homes in sprawling cookie-cutter developments.

The idea of a sustainable community challenges us to envision how we would truly like to live our lives. This vision can be extended to include all people and all communities. Sustaining a healthy, happy, and prosperous lifestyle is the ultimate goal of sustainability. Envisioning this future and choosing how we are to live our lives is also the ultimate goal of ethics.

Endnotes

1 *"The Fortune at the Bottom of the Pyramid: Eradicating Poverty through Profits"* by C.K. Prahalad (Upper Saddle River, NJ: Wharton School Publishing) 2005, pp. 1–3.

2 I owe much of my thinking on sustainable marketing to Patrick Murphy, both through personal correspondence and his essay "Sustainable Marketing," delivered to a conference on "Business and Environmental Sustainability," University of Minnesota Carlson School of Management, April 16, 2005 and, as yet, unpublished.

3 Murphy "Sustainable Marketing"

4 Sustainable marketing seems a growing field within both business and the academic community. Two of the earliest books in this field, both of which remain very helpful, are: *Environmental Marketing: Strategies, Practice, Theory, and Research*, Polonsky, Michael J. and Alma T. Mintu-Wimsatt, eds., Binghampton, NY: The Haworth Press (New York, 1995) and Donald Fuller, *Sustainable Marketing: Managerial-Ecological Issues* (Thousand Oaks, CA: SAGE Publications, 1999). A particularly helpful essay in the Polonsky book is by Seth, Jagdish N. and Atul

Parvatiyar "Ecological Imperatives and the Role of Marketing," pp. 3–20. Seth and Parvatiyar are often credited with coining the term "sustainable marketing" in this essay.

5 KPMG website, http://www.kpmg.ca/en/industries/enr/energy/globalSustain ability Reports.html, May 7, 2005.

6 Some early and creative work on sustainability and banking can be found in "Sustainable Finance and Banking," by Marcel Jeuken (2001). Other work can be found at www.sustainability-in-finance.com

7 See *Banker to the Poor: Micro-Lending and the Battle Against World Poverty* by Muhammad Yunus (University Press Limited, Dhaka, Bangladesh) 2005, and C.K. Prahalad, *The Fortune at the Bottom of the Pyramid*, op. cit., pp. 73–76.

8 See, for example, the video "*Escape from Affluenza*," produced by KTCS, public television, and available from Bullfrog Films. In addition, "simplicity study circles," many of which begin in the workplace, are described in Cecile Andrews, *The Circle of Simplicity* (New York, HarperCollins, 1997).

9 See http://www.smartgrowth.org/default.asp for many helpful resources on the smart growth movement.

Index